Lullabies
and
Nightmares

Dr. Frederick Roberts

LULLABIES AND NIGHTMARES

Copyright © 1998
by
Dr. Frederick Roberts

ISBN 0-925168-58-0

Library of Congress Cataloging-in-Publication Data

In progress

North Country Books, Inc.
311 Turner Street
Utica, New York 13501

Dedication

Lullabies and Nightmares is dedicated to my wife, Ann. She has weathered the many crises in my struggle to be a physician. We were a team from the beginning and she juggled child-raising and husband-consoling along with the host of other duties she had. Our children came in second to my patients as well. Despite the sacrifices, it has been a wonderful journey—a voyage into the mysteries of caring for children. There have been no boring moments.

—Dr. Frederick Roberts, 1998

Contents

CHAPTER 1

❧

Tarnished Halo

It started with a lawsuit. Proceedings had begun and it wasn't clear whether I'd win or lose. All of the uncertainties that lay ahead made me shiver. There was a mystery to be solved and it needed to be done quickly.

I walked into my lawyer's office. Tim rose to greet me. His office was a reflection of his personality. Conservative furniture; books floor to ceiling in the dark mahogany bookcases; pictures of some famous politicians and a few of his family made easy conversation pieces.

He wasn't ready for my outburst.

"Exhume the body, Tim. Get a court order so we can re-examine him."

He scowled and then said, "That's a wild thing to say. Slow down and think. We're nearly ready to go to trial. How come you didn't ask for it earlier?"

"I was in a daze, I guess. Never imagined anybody would sue me."

"Well, that's the climate in today's society."

He put his hand on my shoulder and said, "You don't have to worry. They don't have much of a case. There was no malpractice. Trust me."

I looked at my counselor. He exuded confidence. Here was the cream of the profession telling me not to worry. But he wasn't accused of causing wrongful death. Wrongful death. What a term! To be accused of being responsible for the death of a three-year-old child. My God, how that hurt!

"Tim," I said, "It's not enough to win if this goes to trial. The child was poisoned. The flu didn't kill him. He was poisoned and we can prove it."

My lawyer's interest was aroused, but he wasn't ready to follow my suggestion that the body be examined once more. He walked to his desk and pulled the pretrial transcript from his briefcase. He searched line after line, then looked up at me.

1

"Where's your evidence?" he asked softly. "This testimony has nothing about poison. Not a word. There's no way I would have missed that. Something solid. That's what I need before I dare ask for an exhumation."

The details of the child's quick, fatal illness were fixed in my memory. Howie came home from nursery school and went right to bed. He didn't want supper and when coaxed to drink, began to vomit. The vomiting came in waves every fifteen minutes and was followed by watery diarrhea. He was listless and wrung-out. When his temperature shot up, his mother called me. She did not want me to see him, so I prescribed some simple remedies and advised her to get in touch if anything changed. She agreed and I didn't hear from them until three days later, when an urgent summons came from the hospital.

Apparently, Howie had perked up within a day. He wasn't fully recovered, and it was decided to keep him out of school a little longer. Their next door neighbor, Carl, was a favorite of all the children on the block. He was a retired gardener who enjoyed puttering around in his yard and loved to have someone around to listen to his stories and help pass a few idle hours. He'd let his young friends climb behind the wheel of his old truck, honk the horn and pretend to drive. He'd teach them the names of all of the flowers; let them dig a patch for a row of carrots or corn. That done, they would get a chance to hold the garden hose and saturate everything in sight.

It was a safe haven. Carl put his arm around his small apprentice and they walked to the garage together. They were an interesting pair. Howie, dressed in jacket, woolen trousers, scarf and hat with ear laps, trudging beside his companion, whose outfit was more in keeping with the warm spring day. Carl inspected the equipment they needed for the morning's tasks. He tightened some bolts, squirted oil at the rusty spots and made sure things were in working order. Howie's mother noticed how frail and bent over the old man had become. There was energy in the way he moved, though, and she admired how busy the two of them were as they spread grass seed from one end of the lawn to the other. She went back to her housework and didn't realize that Carl was called to the phone. During that short absence, I learned later, Howie wandered into the garage and saw a bottle of liquid on one of the shelves. It was an open soft drink bottle and when he reached for it, he spilled some on his clothes and some on the floor.

When Carl finished his call, he saw the boy scrambling to put the half-empty bottle back on the shelf. Carl wiped up the mess, cleaned Howie's hands with a rag and they went back to their garden chores. After the seed had been sprinkled over the full extent of the lawn, Carl reached in his pocket for a chocolate bar. One loaded with almonds. Howie took one nibble and began to shake. His face grew pale and he was sick again. This time large amounts of vomit, similar to coffee grounds, gushed from his mouth. He started to sob, headed toward home, but fell to the ground.

The shaken neighbor picked up the limp boy and carried him home. Howie was ashen, barely breathing and still. His mother screamed in terror when Carl placed the child on the sofa.

"Carl, Carl . . . call the doctor. His number's taped on the phone."

She tried to get some response from Howie. His eyes opened, drifted without making contact. He didn't respond to her frantic pleas to talk.

Carl raced back. "I can't get through. Line's busy. Tried him twice."

"Get the ambulance . . . the rescue squad . . . get somebody," she begged.

They were waiting at the door when help came. The crew swept Howie into the ambulance, secured an oxygen mask to his face and called ahead to the hospital. His mother sat alongside and watched as the attendants started intravenous fluids, hooked up the monitors and blasted the siren in their rush to the emergency room.

He was comatose when I arrived. His blood pressure had dropped, his pulse was a feeble flicker. An unusual scent clung to his clothing. I couldn't quite place it.

Howie was surrounded by groups of doctors, nurses, laboratory technicians. Everyone had a role to play.

"Doctor, what's wrong with him?" she implored. "He was fine when he went out to play. Now this. Help him."

She watched as we tried to reverse his state of shock. Howie's skin grew mottled and a flood of bloody mucus seeped from his rectum. Then a flat line appeared on the EKG monitor. He was dead.

Howie's father had arrived shortly before the end. His arms surrounded his wife in tight embrace as if to shield her from the impact of their loss.

I could not intrude on their sorrow. I waited while they lingered at the bedside. The gadgets that couldn't guide us through their son's crisis were removed.

She touched his face, held his hand, kissed his forehead for the last time. Howie's stricken father didn't try to wipe the flow of tears from his cheeks. Then his fury erupted. He turned to me and demanded answers.

I found a nearby conference room and began to review this unbelievable morning. I had faced death many times before but most often there were hints that the patient was slipping away. There was a chance to prepare the family for the inevitable.

"He went so fast," I started. "We couldn't keep his pressure up. Nothing helped. There's no explanation yet."

"What do you mean yet?" yelled the father. "You're the doctor. An expert with children. Don't you know?"

I understood his feelings. "The tests don't give us instant answers. Some we get right away, others take days."

"Then what good are they?"

"They lead the way . . . if we have time."

"You talk about needing time," he went on. "Why couldn't you keep a healthy little boy alive until you could fix him up? He didn't have a worn-out heart . . . never really been sick before. He was feeling better when I left for work this morning."

He paused. "What's the use? Nothing matters now. Howie's gone." He took his wife's arm. "We might as well go home. No point in staying here."

I stopped them. "Better sit a bit longer. We have to talk about signing the certificate."

"You know what to put down. That damn virus infection killed our boy. The one you thought needed only a couple of days of rest."

"Possibly," I said. "But I don't think we know for sure. A postmortem, an autopsy is needed in cases of sudden, unexplained death. It's the law."

She answered first. "Doctor, I can't believe that any of this has happened. I don't know what to say. Dear God. An autopsy. My baby."

Howie's father couldn't control his feelings any longer. He drew his wife close to him and their chorus of sorrow filled the room. They remained locked in their grief, overwhelmed by their catastrophe, until the quiet voice of the hospital chaplain broke through. He had been called to the emergency room when the rush of events took place and then followed us to the private room. His words of consolation calmed them somewhat. They discussed the need for the autopsy with the minister and indicated they would consent.

On impulse, Howie's mother ran toward the room where the body still lay. She found the nursing supervisor.

"I can't go in there again" she said. "But please do this for me. Before it's too late. Snip off some of his ringlets. Snip some off and put them in an envelope. There's nothing else I can keep."

"Of course. I'll be right back. Those locks are so beautiful." She scurried down the hall and came back with the packet of hair. The weeping mother held the envelope close to her and left the hospital with her husband.

The nurse stared after the departing couple. The veteran of daily dealings with car accidents, burn victims, child abuse cases, even murders, turned to me.

"Just think, Doctor, she asked me for a part of her son to take home . . . all that she could have was a few curls. Nobody ever asked for anything like that before."

I called the parents several days later. The gross report was full of non-specific findings that could have been the result of viral or bacterial infections or even chemical toxins. The definitive answer would have to await the microscopic analysis . . another four to six weeks.

They accepted my information without comment. I assured them I would meet with them when the tissue reports were finished. They would be able to ask any questions then.

Howie's father added an unsettling remark before hanging up the phone.

"You're right. That's just a lot of medical jargon. Makes a layman, like me, wonder a bit. Maybe you'll be hearing from us before too long."

The obvious conclusion that he had been talking to a lawyer was confirmed when I received a request in the mail for a copy of all records concerning Howie, from birth to death.

A sinking feeling that pushed logic away wouldn't disappear. I discussed the little boy's sad history with my wife and my colleagues. I asked them to be unrelenting in their review of the cycle of events that ended Howie's life. There was a comforting unanimity in their assessment. They reasoned it was a quirk of fate that this child succumbed to his illness. There were no clues; nothing different in his case. They classified me as blameless.

But I could not be as merciful. Doubts began to erode my feelings of innocence. Had I overlooked something? Could he have been saved?

The subpoena stirred things up. I contacted my lawyer and we mapped a strategy for my defense. The medical experts retained by my insurance carrier went over all the available evidence and concluded that there had been no culpable acts on my part. They urged that we defend against the allegations of malpractice.

Months went by without further response from the other side. I was encouraged momentarily. Maybe they realized they had acted in haste and had struck out blindly. Vengeance for their child's death. Their suffering and mine continued during the lull in the legal process. I'm sure that my nights were as restless as theirs, and I prayed that the ordeal would be over so that we could get our lives back on track again.

We were notified at last that an examination before trial would be held. In preparation for this phase of our battle, my attorney fired mock questions at me, to acquaint me with our opponent's tactics.

"Just stick to the facts," Tim advised me. "You know much more about this case than anyone else. Stay cool, Doctor. They'll try to make you lose your temper. And another thing, don't be too technical. No big words . . . plain English will be more effective."

A stenographer, witnesses for each side and the attorneys gathered in a large chamber in their office. I wanted to run over and tell the parents how sorry I was that Howie was lost to them . . . that I understood their anguish. Instead, I looked at the two of them, saw the vacant expression in their eyes, and forgave them for the wounds they were inflicting on me.

Once started, the testimony went swiftly. Their lawyer didn't manage to rattle me. We weren't blown away by any damning statements. I finally sat back in my chair, underarms drenched with sweat, but satisfied I had told my story convincingly.

The hearing droned on. There were examinations of the parents, the ambulance personnel, the emergency room staff. Repetition followed repetition. Nothing unexpected until Carl, their neighbor, was questioned.

Then I heard the words that solved the mystery. A soft drink bottle. The one that Howie spilled. That explained the peculiar aroma I noticed in the emergency room. Perhaps he drank from that bottle!

I scribbled a note and handed it to my lawyer, but Carl had been excused already before he glanced at my comments. No matter. There would be time to prove my theory later.

That night I couldn't sleep. But my wakefulness was spent checking possible poisons that could have acted with such speed. I made out a list and with it ruled out natural causes for the child's death.

"Tim," I said, later in the week, after I'd read as many books on forensic medicines and poisons as I could find, "When I talked about opening up the grave, that shook you up, didn't it?"

Without waiting for an answer, I went on.

"It would be cruel . . . very unfeeling. Even you think it would be eerie. Good. That gives us the leverage we need."

"Doc, you've lost me. I haven't any idea what you're talking about."

"Here goes. I wrote you a note during the pretrial. Remember? But you had finished your questioning and didn't even pick it up. I wanted you to know that I had figured out the solution to our case."

My lawyer pulled his chair up and waited for my explanation.

"During the neighbor's testimony, there was a part where he told about Howie spilling something from a bottle onto his clothes and the floor of the garage. I figure that he drank a little first, dumped some by accident . . . but, Tim, here's the point. He swallowed enough of the stuff to be poisoned."

"Whew, you may be right! But how do we prove it?"

"I thought about that, too. Here are some ideas. That bottle might have been filled with an insecticide. Carl was a school custodian before he retired. It could have been 2-4-D or arsenic or something similar. The way Howie acted, it was most likely arsenic. Quick and deadly, all that bleeding from his intestines and the collapse of his blood pressure."

"We need a sample," Tim added. "We can ask to have it analyzed. I'll see what their counsel has to say."

"That would do it, but there's one hitch. Carl may say that he didn't see the boy drink anything. That's why I brought up the threat of exhumation. Carl is a gentle guy . . . he was nearly in tears at the hearing . . . he was close to the family. He wouldn't want them to go through all that just to prove our point."

"Maybe not. But this theory of yours. If you had known about the bottle in the garage the day he died, what tests could have been done? Do you find it in the blood only? Anywhere else?"

"I've learned a lot about arsenic since I became suspicious. It's been around for years . . . been used in murder . . . but there's a great deal of it around commercially . . . even in the average person's home."

"No fooling. You'd think it would be outlawed."

"Probably should be. Dangerous for kids. You've seen those ant buttons, haven't you? They put them under sinks . . . arsenic trioxide. Rose bush sprays and other garden supplies. Some are loaded with arsenic . . . not all."

"Easy access, eh? For a child who couldn't read a label. My own son puts everything in his mouth. He has to be watched all the time."

"Absolutely. And let me bore you with a couple of other facts. The dose by mouth to kill an adult, if it's arsenic trioxide, is 180 milligrams or so. And for a child about one fifth of that could kill him quickly, just like Howie. If you are looking for arsenic early on, you collect stomach contents or the urine. Later the blood, skin, hair, nails and the stools will show levels . . . weeks or months after a toxic dose."

"How about Howie's case?"

"That's where I've got to ask you to bluff a little. This poor child lived no more than five or six hours after he got hold of the soft drink bottle. If we can analyze that liquid, we won't have to petition for hair samples or ask to open the grave."

"You said they had snipped off some of the boy's hair. Isn't that all we need?"

"My reading says it shows up in the portions of the hair closest to the scalp within thirty hours after the toxic dose. If we can nudge Carl a little . . . if he thinks the parents prize those few strands of hair so much . . . maybe he'll give us our evidence."

"Worth a try. I'll get started. As I said, their attorney's a pretty reasonable guy."

I had a sense of relief. "If only this were finished," I confided. "I used to be a fairly relaxed person until this rotten case took over my life. I loved to be with patients, but lately there always seems to be a lawsuit hanging over my head. That two-way trust is gone."

"Knock if off, Fred. You guys were sacred cows . . . untouchables. In this case you were right. But you fellows do make mistakes."

I knew the debate was endless. Even my lawyer thought we all had tarnished halos.

Our gambit worked. Tim had lunch with the other lawyer. They came to an agreement over a couple of martinis. Carl was not anxious, at first, to turn the bottle over to the toxicologist. But when he learned that we had indirect methods of checking for ingested drugs, he permitted the analysis. He said again and again he didn't think Howie could have drunk anything before he spilled fluid on his clothes and the floor. The poor fellow was nearly overcome with remorse. He prayed something other than his oversight was responsible for Howie's death.

When I received two calls the following week, my ordeal was over. Large amounts of an arsenic salt were found by the police laboratory. The probable role of this chemical was so strong that the plaintiff's attorney recommended the case be dropped.

Howie's parents asked to talk to me. They apologized for their use of the courts in dealing with their grief. I was the only target they could identify. I guess everyone needs a punching bag as an outlet for hostility.

It was time to look back and see how my commitment to medicine and the care of children began. How different the climate was then.

CHAPTER 2

֍

The Search for Beginnings

The sights, smells and events of my father's office carried a great attraction for me. My daydreams weren't about space ships or swimming the Hellespont, but were aimed at stethoscopes and scalpels.

My family lived in an apartment over my father's office. Sometimes I would creep down the long spiral staircase, park myself on the bottom step and watch the progression of patients into the waiting room. They would search for a spot to sit until their turn came. There were no appointments but they knew that the doctor would stay until everyone had been cared for, unless he was called to deliver a baby or manage a hospital emergency. They gathered, an assortment of walk-in sufferers, content to have their ailments brought to the doctor's attention, no matter how long the delay. Some came alone, others carried a child or were the companion of an ailing parent.

Although the years have blurred some of the details, my memory still highlights certain features of that waiting area. It was a spacious room with a high ceiling and large windows. Along one wall were several padded benches in tandem; a cluster of straight-backed chairs was placed near another wall, and two wooden masterpieces flanked the fireplace. They were oak chairs, carved with intricate designs by some unsung craftsman.

The mantelpiece always had a vase with fresh flowers, some bric-a-brac and the classic, framed reprint of the doctor at a patient's bedside. A small table heaped with magazines, several lamps, a brass umbrella stand, coatracks and a frayed rug made up the rest of the furnishings.

The entrance to the consultation room was guarded by large sliding doors. At intervals they would be opened. A patient would leave and my father would look out among the assemblage, beckon to one, smile at the rest and return to his mysterious inner office.

That inner office was most intriguing. He worked alone. No staff to attend to minor details. There were gleaming instruments in the white, glass-doored cabinets. Bottles of pills to be dispensed; cough concoctions; worm remedies; packages of plaster of Paris for setting fractures; aromatic antiseptics; boxes of gauze; yards of adhesive tape; obstetrical forceps—all assigned a place. As a rule a sterilizer was boiling in one area, filled with syringes and needles.

His desk was a massive structure. Several medical journals were usually in view, as well as the telephone, a notebook, a blood pressure manometer, prescription pads and an inkstand. His stethoscope was draped around his neck much of the time. A metal examining table, equipped with stirrups for the gynecology patients, was tucked against the outer wall. Directly overhead, a sealed beam light provided good visibility for the minor surgical cases.

Sometimes I'd fall asleep at the bottom of the stairs. Long after the last patient had been treated, my father would find me there, lift me up and carry me to bed, possibly to dream of a future life as a doctor.

There were other influences pulling me toward the healing arts. We lived next door to the medical school. My brother and I would watch the students on their way to and from classes. Often they would stop and talk with us, telling us about some of their interesting experiences. We would listen, fascinated by the stories, wondering if we would ever take part in their glamorous world. One of the upper classmen was our uncle. He, too, spun tales that were thrilling; that involved rescues from death; cures for strange-sounding diseases; stories about machines that could see inside the body; about a new treatment for diabetes, insulin, that could control the body's mixed-up sugar metabolism. This was a time in history when no one had flown around the world; an interval between two world wars. My heroes wore masks and gowns and rubber gloves, and the operating room was their battlefield.

One day I was assigned the job of helping my mother with the laundry. The process was beneath the dignity of an aspiring surgeon and my mind drifted from the humdrum work at hand. I ignored the safety rules and held onto the sheet as it was being fed through the wringer of our washing machine. I felt a shearing pain as my index finger was drawn between the rollers. My screams brought my mother rushing into the room. She turned off the motor, released a lever and was able to free me from my entanglement. There was near amputation of my fingertip. It hung loosely, a bloody, mean-looking appendage.

"Your Dad's out on call somewhere. I can't reach him." She yelled for my older brother, sent him down to the office for a gauze bandage and tried to calm me down. Stabbing sensations exploded from my injured finger.

"See if your Uncle Mannie is in class," she commanded my brother. "Bring him here as quickly as you can."

She turned to me to offer some consolation. "You'll be fine. Mannie will fix you up. Now lie still. Put you hand on the pillow and rest until he gets here."

A local anesthetic and a dozen or more sutures restored my finger to normal. My faith in medicine was undiminished, but I wasn't so sure about surgery.

The allure of the medical school was irresistible to an eight-year-old. The students invited me to inspect the many artifacts on display in the lobby of the college. An historical journey from the time of Hippocrates to the modern era gave me an overview of scientific progress. A few of the shelves were a little frightening and my guides hurried me past the jars of fetuses and surgical specimens. They introduced me to the morgue attendant and wondered aloud if I was ready to comb the hair on one of the cadavers. My courage faltered and I escaped as quickly as I could, more than willing to wait until I was a full-fledged student.

My first memories of the effect of trust on the healing process took place when I was a young child. I had been coughing and running a fever, feeling quite miserable with my affliction, acute bronchitis. The pre-scribed treatments weren't working and I needed some additional boost to correct my symptoms. I lay in bed, feeling very sorry for myself, and could not imagine that I would ever be better.

I waited impatiently for my father to return to the office and assure me that I was not doomed, that in time I would be able to play ball and do other things healthy kids could do.

The day dragged on; my spirits grew fainter and fainter until I heard a sound in the driveway—the crunch of our old Packard on the stone-paved road.

There was a pause. The side door opened to murmurings below. Then a familiar step on the stairs. I could hear the coins jingling in his pocket as he hurried toward me.

The door swung wide. There was my Dad. He had a dish of French vanilla ice cream, a sports magazine, a smile and a reassuring look that let me know my survival was guaranteed.

The healing arts were certainly not found in the miserable tasting cough medicines, the chest rubs, the vaporizer or the aspirin. Softness of speech, an unfurrowed brow, an aura of hope, I learned, were necessities in the sick room. My recovery from a minor respiratory infection was hastened by faith in the doctor.

My interest in medicine was not applauded by everyone in the family. My mother tried hard to conceal her opposition. She wanted me to have a wide range of options. She was sitting in our new kitchen, perched on a tall stool. A textbook was propped in front of her and she was kneading dough for strudel while testing my language skills. We had moved to a residential neighborhood several miles from the office, and now my brothers and I could quarrel, even practice our music, without worrying about the noise.

"*Agricola*," my mother offered.

"That's farmer," I said.

"*Amicus*."

"Friend."

"*Puella*."

"Girl."

"*Puer*."

"Boy."

"Keep stirring," advised my mother. "If you want to make smooth ice cream, you have to churn and churn."

"I'm doing the best I can. But it's boring."

"It may be boring but you and your brothers will finish the whole batch for dessert. There won't be a drop left."

We were getting ready for the weekend. I drew the kitchen assignment this time. That meant peeling carrots, shucking corn, mixing cake batter and tasting the end pieces of strudel. The clean-up operation was part of the duty also. The final indignity was mopping the linoleum until it sparkled. In spite of the bonus of coating some of the strudel with the leavings of freshly-made ice cream, I would have traded with my older brother and trimmed the bushes or cut the lawn.

The best part of the chores was the chance to learn Latin. My mother tried to take my mind off the menial part of my duties. She drilled me in grammar and vocabulary so that I would have a friendship with Latin when I added that to my curriculum in the fall.

"It's the basis for the romance languages as well as English. If you can master Latin, the others will be a cinch."

"You need it for med school, too, Mom."

"Are you sure you want to be a doctor? Look how hard your father works. We never see him." Then with an air of resignation she said, "Tonight. Watch him tonight. We've made this great meal for him. Everything he loves. He'll sit down, put his spoon to his mouth and the phone will ring. He'll feel guilty but he'll give me a kiss, apologize and dash off. How can I ask him to finish his dinner first? I have to share him with his darn patients!"

"You wouldn't want him to be any different, would you?"

"You bet I would. I'd like to live a normal life . . . like everybody else. I want it for you, too. At fourteen it might seem glamorous . . . what your Dad does. But Fred, when you have a family, that has to be time for them, too."

"But it's all I ever wanted to be."

"I might as well get used to it then, if your mind is made up. Be sure you give yourself a chance, though, to try other things."

"I have," I reminded her. "Let's see, I've ruled out concert pianist."

She smiled. Eight years of piano lessons from a tolerant teacher and I could play two or three selections with mediocrity.

"I must admit that you aren't a gifted musician. When I was pregnant with you, I used to listen to Brahms and Tchaikovsky. Only the masters. I thought maybe it'd rub off on you. Someday you'd play at Carnegie Hall. Instead, your music teacher finally gave up. She wouldn't take any more money for your lessons . . . you were hopeless."

"How about sketching? That was no better."

She agreed. I lacked talent in the arts with the exception of writing. I had enjoyed reading my compositions to the family but I knew that they were generous critics. I knew I wouldn't change . . still wanted to be a doctor.

The most magnetic force at work was the occasional trip with Dad to a patient's home. He'd invite me to ride with him when he had to visit a sick family. This was a chance to learn how a doctor responded to people in trouble. He'd fill my head with stories of other calls; about the times he had been stuck in snow banks during a blizzard; of twins and even triplets that he had delivered at home; of gunshot wounds and farm accidents that needed treatment on the spot.

"Something different every day, Fred," he'd tell me. "You never know what you'll run into. You've got to be prepared because you'll be all alone and they're depending on you."

One story had a profound effect on me. We were driving to a patient's home in one of the more densely-populated parts of the city. Working people and some elderly retirees mainly lived there, in houses crammed tightly together. Some places had garages, others small storage sheds. The lawns were mowed neatly and most had gardens. One old black man grew the tallest sunflowers I had ever seen. Dad always stopped and kidded with him. They would laugh and trade jokes for a time until my father would realize that a sick patient was waiting. He'd pull out his gold pocket watch, point to it and announce, "Sam, I've got my boy with me today. He's learning my trade. Better teach him to be punctual."

Sam would pull his elbow off the rolled-down window and step back. "Hold it, Doc," he'd say. "Take some of these beauties home to your missus." A bunch of his prize flowers would always end up with us. I listened to that routine many times. It never varied. Even the parting words to me, "Sonny, your dad's a great doctor. Nobody like him." Then, "See you next week, Doc. At the office."

"He used to be a fighter. At the arena downtown. I told you that I was the doctor at ringside for years. Well, Sam was awfully good. He was a middleweight. Fought most of the big names. His only weakness was that he cut easily. Sometimes I had to stop the fight. He'd get a head butt and open up that scar tissue. Couldn't let him get ruined for the couple of bucks they paid in those days. He understood, but he'd beg me to sew him up myself. He said I did a better job than the doctor near his house. That guy didn't like to work on the coloreds. Can you beat that?"

He slowed the car down. "Remind me to tell you about the little girl who lives in that house. Must be pretty grown up now."

He wouldn't forget a story. I looked at the freshly-painted Cape Cod. I didn't realize how much it would mean to me a few years later. But I wanted to hear more about Sam and his career.

"The rest of it? Sure. Sam needed the money. So we had to mend those cuts quickly. I had to certify the fighters before they could go in the ring again after a technical knockout. It was lucky that Sam healed faster than most. He kept at it until he was nearly forty. Took on all comers. That's why we go through our little routine. He loves to talk about the old times. He knows your mother likes those sunflowers, too, and he'll expect to see them on the mantelpiece the next time he comes to our office."

I waited in the car while my father made his call on a woman who had gall bladder colic. It was nearly an hour before the medication gave her relief. On the way back he told me about the time he took care of the girl in the Cape Cod house.

We drew up alongside their house. My father stopped the car. He reached for a cigarette, lit it and leaned back. He blew a few smoke rings toward the dashboard and sighed.

It was a tough case, let me tell you. We didn't have the kind of hospitals that we do now. I wouldn't dare treat someone as sick as the little Burdick girl at home these days. But I had no other choice.

I think it was sometime in January or early February. It had been bitterly cold and I hoped nobody would need me that night. The car had been hard to start. We had to crank them to get going back then. I just wanted to sit down, take my shoes off and relax.

Your mother took the message. She hated to bother me but it sounded serious. She knew the Burdicks didn't scare easily.

So I was on my way. Mrs. Burdick was looking out the window and let me in. I didn't have to knock. She told me to hang my coat and hat on the hooks in the hall. She said she was sorry to call me so late but her daughter was getting worse by the minute. She pushed the other children away from the door but they regrouped right away. They climbed on chairs and on the tables . . didn't want to miss a thing, I guess. I'd never been called to their house before but Ann had never been so sick. Ann was the baby of the family . . . the youngest of seven kids and she was struggling.

Mrs. Burdick looked haggard and worn. She told my father that Ann had suddenly gotten worse. Usually she took care of things herself . . . with all those kids . . . who could afford to call the doctor? She'd give them a hot drink, rub some Vicks on the chest or put on a flannel wrap. But not this time. Even her husband was worried. He was the one who made her call.

"She's been sickly . . . one cold right after another . . . ," the girl's mother went on to tell me. "The older ones were never like that. I can't figure out what is wrong."

I told her that Ann probably was at the age where she picked up infections at school, that they pass germs around very easily. All this time Mr. Burdick hadn't said a word but he gestured for me to follow him into the bedroom where Ann was propped up on pillows. She was leaning forward, her chest sucked in with every breath . . . making a croaking sound. There was a look of terror on her face. She was too weak even to say hello to me.

I opened my bag and got out my stethoscope. The light wasn't very good so Mr. Burdick produced a floor lamp that could be focused right on Ann. Poor kid. There was a cold sweat on her cheeks and forehead and a touch of blue around her lips. Her pulse was racing so fast that I could scarcely count it.

Her parents stood near the side of her bed as I examined her. It was obvious that this child was in deep trouble. I managed to look at her throat and saw there was a thick, grayish membrane covering her tonsils and the back wall of the throat.

"Can you talk, Ann?" I asked her. "Can you talk?"

She shook her head and her breathing became deeper.

"I can't," she whispered to me. "I can't. It hurts so!"

I turned to Mr. Burdick and asked him to come with me. We went out in the hallway and I advised him to send the other children to their rooms. They were excited but they couldn't be allowed to stay. That's when I said that we had to do something for Ann very soon or it would be too late.

He asked me what was causing the sudden emergency. I told him that Ann had diphtheria. I explained that her pulse was weak and that her heart could give out if she had to keep working so hard to get air; that there was a membrane blocking her windpipe and that I'd have to place a tube in her throat and then get some antitoxin in her as soon as possible.

You can bet that there was action when he heard that. The other children were hustled away and Mr. Burdick and I carried Ann out to the kitchen table. He couldn't get over how quickly her condition had changed . . . she was fine last night he kept saying.

I told him I'd explain everything later but that now we had to hurry. I sent him for a sheet and a blanket, and we wrapped her good and tight and sat her up on the kitchen table, leaning forward . . . that way she'd get air better.

I had to ask him to hold her so she couldn't wiggle. I kept my voice down to a whisper so Ann wouldn't hear everything. Most of it was with gestures. I washed my hands quickly, then took an O'Dwyer tube from its case. This tube has to be placed in the back of her throat, I said, right down into the windpipe. If I couldn't do it, I'd have to make a hole in her trachea . . . I pointed just below the Adam's apple.

Mr. Burdick held on as tightly as he could. He closed his eyes and prayed. I could feel his hands stiffen. All the while Mrs. Burdick kept stroking Ann and reassuring her that she would be all right. I placed my finger in the back of the child's throat, felt for the opening of the windpipe and guided the instrument past the obstruction. I checked to make sure it was where it belonged and then taped the upper end of the tube to her face with a strip of adhesive.

Ann began to cough. Her eyes almost popped out of her head. She looked as if she was suffering. Then she coughed up a big plug of mucus and her breathing seemed easier.

She's going to make it, I remember saying. Fred, I was sure that she would. I squeezed Ann's hand . . . put my ear right next to that tube . . . had to make sure it was working. Then I rattled off a bunch of orders. They were to get a kettle going and keep it boiling. The room had to be moist so the mucus secretions wouldn't cake and block the lifeline. The other kids would have to be kept out of the way. The room had to be dark and Ann would have sleep right on the table.

I looked at those poor, tired parents and said that they were going to be kept very busy. I explained that they'd need to sit near Ann and make sure she didn't get her hands loose. If that tube ever got pulled out, she would suffocate.

I made sure they knew what they had to do and then I headed to the door, telling them that I'd go for the diphtheria antitoxin and be right back.

It was only a short drive to the pharmacy at the contagious disease hospital. I got hold of the antitoxin, hurried back to the Burdick house and gave Ann her first dose. She had shown a little improvement and had fallen asleep once her breathing was easier.

We sat in the kitchen with the light turned down low and watched. Ann opened her eyes finally and looked around. She tried to get free from the strait-jacket gadget we had her in but gave up and fell back to sleep again.

Mrs. Burdick insisted that I get some rest. She cleared a space on the sofa for me and I dropped off to sleep for maybe twenty or thirty minutes, then I got up and went back to the kitchen to watch Ann's progress.

Mr. Burdick sat there quietly, cradling a large glass of hot tea in his hands. He reached for a sugar cube, put it in his mouth and sipped slowly. We waited together for the morning. Both of us were relieved that all was stable. We watched the calm up and down movement of Ann's chest, so different from the distress of early morning. Mrs. Burdick rushed around meanwhile, getting the older children ready for school, until I told her the house was under quarantine. All seven children would have to stay home until the health department allowed them to go back to class.

We talked for hours, Mr. Burdick and I. He confessed that he hadn't trusted doctors before tonight. An older brother of Ann's, one of twins, had died of pneumonia. They had called a doctor then, but he had stalled about coming to the house and when he did, it was too late.

Ann got better and in a few days, it was safe to remove the tube. She grew stronger daily and I was sure she would recover without complications. The Burdicks were grateful. They're wonderful people . . . not very gushy. But they knew how close they came to losing Ann. They asked to pay their bill. Fred, you'll find it hard to put a price on your work . . . if you decide to be a doctor. I studied them and said there had been five days and nights of care, the serum, placing of the tube. I'd have to make it fifty dollars.

Fifty dollars? I remember she said they couldn't pay it all at once. Then she reached into the cupboard and pulled out an empty sugar bowl. She found some bills, all crumpled up and placed them in my hand.

"Here's twenty-five dollars, Doctor," she said to me. "And we'll pay the rest off as soon as we can. This is a slow season for carpenters . . . not much construction right now."

Then I told them their Ann was a spunky seven-year-old . . . to be so brave and uncomplaining.

My father had finished his story. He started the car and we were home in no time. Throughout the years I was in high school, I made a great many calls with him and listened to case histories by the score.

During my freshman year in college, a friend arranged a blind date for me. Three couples were going to a dinner dance. The others sat in the car while I rang the door bell. It seemed to me I'd been there before.

I introduced myself to the nice lady who answered the bell.

"I believe your daughter, Ann, is expecting me."

Mrs. Burdick smiled and said that Ann would be ready shortly. Ann's father walked over to me, stuck his hand out and pumped mine vigorously.

"I know your father, young man. Pleased to meet you."

CHAPTER 3

సౌ

The In-Between Years

The career was decided. I would be a physician and follow in my father's path, possibly to practice with him. My preceptorship could be served in familiar surroundings and in time I hoped to acquire some of the extraordinary skills that he possessed by working alongside of him.

The years of medical school were tests of physical endurance and mental resiliency. There were times when the dream seemed to be a blur of muscles, nerves and tendons staring at me from the pages of the anatomy text. The need to commit to memory the intricate details of the human body crowded out any temporal thoughts. I was overcome with guilt if I browsed through the *New York Times Book Review* instead of puzzling over the function of the *corpus striatum*.

I was sick of books. I couldn't wait to see living, breathing people. But everyone was trained with the same tedious exposure to facts. The clinical years were yet to come when we would see patients and try to apply the knowledge that filled the shelves of my library.

I was studying one weekend during my junior year when my father called me. He had been shoveling coal into the furnace, a job that we shared equally. I heard him call out for help. I raced down to the cellar and saw him sitting on a stool, clutching his chest. He reached for my hand and tried to grip it, but then let go and said softly, "I need you. The pain's bad. Help me upstairs. I want to lie down."

His palms were soaking wet, his face had a strange expression and all color had left his cheeks. I tried to support his considerable weight. He was not able to budge at first and looked at me, saying it felt as though someone were sitting on his chest.

We both knew that he was having a coronary. We couldn't find a spot in the damp cellar for him to rest while we sent for the ambulance.

"Get my bag. It's in the car. Need something for this awful pain."

I flew up the stairs, grabbed the black bag and raced to his side. He was breathing heavily, but somehow had a smile for me.

"The morphine tablets are in the small pocket inside the bag. There's a spoon. Hitch it over the alcohol burner. Dissolve one of those in water."

He waited as I fumbled with the burner. The flame heated the water quickly. I sucked up the medication into a glass syringe and poised it uncertainly near his arm.

"Dad, I've never done this before. We've never given shots in class." He beckoned me to hurry. I raised his shirt sleeve, dabbed some alcohol on the skin and pushed the needle home. As gently as I could, I lowered him to the floor.

"This sweater will have to be your pillow for now. I'll cover you with my overcoat and then call the ambulance. I'll sit with you until they get here."

The two of us counted the minutes until he felt some easing of the chest pain. It wasn't too long before the attendants hoisted him onto a stretcher and we headed for the hospital. I sat next to him. He was resting a little, eyes half-closed. He was chilly, in spite of two woolen blankets. We had nearly reached the hospital when he looked up and noticed I was crying.

"You did fine, Fred. It made me feel good to have you there."

They lifted him onto the stretcher and wheeled him directly to the cardiology department where one of his old friends approached him.

"Frank, we'll make you comfortable as soon as we can. I'll do your EKG myself and we'll see what's going on inside you."

It was a feeling, almost like paralysis, to watch my father as a patient. He was not in charge anymore. He lay passively when the electrodes were positioned. The cardiologist, lips set in a tight line, studied the cardiac tracing. He didn't speak to my father, but collected the recordings and signalled to me. We tip-toed to the corner of the room and he whispered to me that it was a coronary occlusion.

"We don't have to tell him. He knows. But we'll get him upstairs to the cardiac section. We'll keep him there and see what happens over the next few days."

I had a feeling as though some powerful suction was pulling his life and mine. It was a tug-of-war we couldn't win. I followed the trail of interns, orderlies and nurses to the elevator and to his room.

My next duty was to be with my mother. She would have gotten home by now. How to tell her about the morning's events without letting my fear show? I blundered through it without too much emotion and we spent the night taking turns at his bedside. She refused to think that anything could endanger him. He was indestructible; the one she relied on; the leader of the family.

His illness lasted nearly a month. It appeared as though he was better. Every noon I'd pull a chair near his bed and have lunch with him. He'd have his bland hospital diet and I'd munch on a roast beef or turkey sandwich. He'd watch in envy as I polished off my meal and promised me that he'd be home, raiding the refrigerator before long. He missed my mother's cooking and the ambience of home.

We talked for hours about how he would slow down when he was better. Work just enough to keep the practice going until I could join him. He was permitted to sit in a chair and even answer some of the dozens of cards his patients mailed him. My mother sent his best suit along in preparation for his discharge and insisted that the barber cut and groom his hair.

We often reviewed some of the more interesting cases I'd been assigned in my clerkship at medical school. He used to enjoy figuring out the best way to manage them and then see if his approach matched that of my professors.

"The patient is a forty-year-old white male," I started. "He was in his usual state of health until two days prior to admission when he noticed a painful swelling of the right testicle."

I hesitated. Most often he would fire question after question once I had started the history. Instead, there was a peculiar noise. He made a gurgling sound. The on-duty intern answered my shouts immediately. The intracardiac adrenalin was useless, as I knew it would be.

I had a feeling of dangling in space. My first contact with death. I sat in the corner of the room dreading my next role . . . the messenger of bad news. I called my brothers and had them hurry to the hospital with our mother.

My father's death changed my career plans. There would be no wise preceptor guiding my way. I'd have to sift through the possibilities and decide what route to take. Surgery, radiology, the laboratory sciences had intellectual appeal but lacked the patient-doctor relationship.

Our medical school had an unusual requirement for graduation. Every student had to participate in six home deliveries before he could be granted a degree. A pair of seniors formed a team with an experienced obstetrical nurse and, under the supervision of a practicing physician, provided care during the lying-in period. Women whose previous pregnancies had been uncomplicated could enroll in the clinic and be cared for by our outpatient unit at delivery time.

It worked quite simply. The patient would notify the hospital switchboard when her time was near. The operator then buzzed the obstetrics call room. The students and the graduate nurse assigned to the case would requisition a suitcase from the hospital supply room. With all the paraphernalia needed to conduct a home delivery, we then would go by taxi to the patient's home.

Our call was from Beulah, the wife of Phil, the Woodman. She had five other children; the last two were delivered at home. The family lived in a run-down section of the city, not far from the hospital. It was a dilapidated frame structure. The gutters hung down from the roof, in need of attention. The front steps had several broken treads and the screen door was rusted and torn. A hand-printed sign was fastened to a pillar. It read, "PHIL THE WOODMAN." Piles of logs were littered over the porch and alongside the house.

Phil greeted us at the door. He was a short, stout man in his early forties. Thinning hair, florid complexion, a small moustache, protruding ears and a receding chin made his features unforgettable.

He said, "She's right on time. 'Sposed to be today, and, by golly, it is."

He took our heavy suitcase and carried it into the house. He stared at us intently, scratched his head and spoke to the nurse.

"They're younger every time. Hope they know what they're doing. The last guys, though, did a good job. No troubles at all."

Beulah was diapering her two-year-old. She smiled when she saw us.

"Don't mind him. He just likes to hear himself talk. Nice to meet you doctors. I know Miss Westcott. She's been here before."

She waddled into the kitchen, sat down, held her safely-diapered toddler on her lap, and said, "I've been having pretty good pains. Shouldn't be too long. The last time . . . a couple of pushes and out came this fellow."

Her husband peeked into the kitchen.

"Beulah, your Ma's here. The kids'll stay with her until tomorrow. I can pick them up after I finish work."

"Great. They'd sure get in the way. The older ones want to watch but I don't think they should, do you?"

"Naw. Plenty of time for that later. Let's get outta here."

We waited until each of the children had been kissed and told to

mind Grandma. Phil loaded everyone into his truck and after a few sputtering misfires, the motor started. They waved and shouted as the truck
left the driveway. Grandma muttered to her son-in-law that she hoped it
would be the last time she'd be needed. He grinned, turned palms up-
ward, raised his shoulders and said nothing.

"Let's get organized," Miss Westcott suggested. "Which one of you
is going to pour ether? The other will have to go over the supplies with
me."

I had lost the coin toss. My partner, Theo, was to catch the baby.
Miss Westcott, briskly efficient, cleared the kitchen table and had us lug
it into the big bedroom. She sprayed some disinfectant on the surface,
draped it and readied the instruments. Theo and I watched the preparation
while Beulah dozed between pains. After the nurse had checked the items
to her satisfaction, she covered the work stand with a sterile sheet.

"Will you help me set up the delivery area? She might fool us and be
in real active labor pretty quick. You know multips."

We carried the rest of the supplies to the side of the bed. Miss Westcott stripped the covers and sheets and placed them in a hamper. A large
rubberized cloth protected the mattress; then some newspapers and a
large cotton pad were layered on top. I found a pail for later use, and my
partner and I waited for further instructions. Miss Westcott was satisfied
with our makeshift labor room. She pulled an anesthesia mask, some
gauze squares, a can of ether and a large safety pin from the suitcase,
snapped the lid shut and slid it our of the way.

"I'll leave this at the top of the bed. Don't worry, you'll have enough
room to work. I've been in lots of homes where it's so crowded we fall
all over each other."

Theo heard a little cry from the next room. He nudged me and we
hurried to the woman's side.

"Hey, it's nothing," Beulah said. "Water just broke. I thought you
oughta know."

Theo tried to be calm. He went to the phone and called our supervis-
ing obstetrician. "No, we haven't examined her yet. It happened just now.
The contractions? About every three to four minutes. I don't think
they're too hard yet."

Miss Westcott was helping our patient into the bedroom. They were
sharing a laugh at the uselessness of men at this juncture. The nurse
pushed us back.

"I'll prep her now. Then you can check the fetal heart and see how she's dilated. I left the gloves and K-Y jelly over there."

"What did he say when you told him about the leaking membranes?" I asked.

"He said he'd be down before long. No reason why we couldn't handle delivering the baby, but he'd be around to back us up."

The two of us walked about as if we were expectant fathers. We hoped that we would be able to handle our responsibilities in a professional manner when the moment came. There was a world of difference in handling life's greatest miracle in these surroundings rather than a modern obstetrical suite, but enough babies arrived in India or Baffin Land without benefit of hospitals. The population projection by the turn of the century was estimated at more than five billion. We consoled each other that we'd do fine.

Miss Westcott interrupted our reveries. "How about listening to the heart and then get gowned and masked. She's moving right along."

I went to the head of the bed while Theo examined Beulah. As I reached for the can of ether and the mask, Beulah shouted, "The baby's coming. The baby's coming!"

Theo reached for a sterile towel. He was set for the Ritgen maneuver. I grabbed the ether and opened the safety pin and pierced the top of the can so that a slow drip could fall on the mask and ease the pangs of childbirth.

I placed the mask over her face to put her to sleep. She thrashed about as the pains reached their peak and pushed my hand away. The ether can fell to the floor.

"Guess Beulah didn't need help from any of us," Miss Westcott said in a low voice.

Theo let the sterile towel drop.

"That's not how it is in the books. I didn't get a chance to do a thing. Boom. There he was."

He reached for the rubber suction bulb and cleared the baby's mouth. I joined him and we looked in awe at the screaming newborn.

Our attending OB man stood in the doorway. He pulled on a pair of gloves, clamped the cord and wrapped the baby in a receiving blanket.

"Here you go, Beulah. Another one. As bald as Phil, but a helluva lot better looking."

She looked at her son. "My mother said it would be a boy. I was stuck way out in front. She swears that means it's a boy."

The experience with Beulah and her labor didn't make obstetrics an attractive goal for Theo or me. I nibbled away at other specialties during my last year as an undergraduate. Ear, nose and throat didn't appeal to me; nor did ophthalmology. I wanted to work on the complete person. Internal medicine caught my fancy and rose to the top of my list. But how about children? Pediatrics was a field just coming into its own. That might be the challenge that I wanted. Of course, the decision would be shared with my new bride.

Ann, the little girl in my father's story, and I were married just before my graduation. We rented an apartment a few blocks from the medical center and set up housekeeping. Ann helped us meet our expenses with her job as a dietician at the hospital. We'd bump into each other during lunch time and manage to share a few moments before our busy schedules made us part.

She had to leave work during my internship, however, when our first baby was nearly due. I was receiving training in Psychiatry and found it very interesting and not nearly so demanding as some of the other specialties. There was an added advantage in that the psychiatric hospital provided a private suite for the intern. Not dormitory style with several roommates the way it was in the other services. A bright, airy room with an innerspring mattress on the bed. Dresser, clothes closet, writing desk and a small radio on the nightstand. But the greatest luxury was the bathtub and shower. An added benefit for hungry physicians in training was the director's tradition of inviting guests for Sunday dinner. We looked forward to spending some time together in the quieter atmosphere of the mental hospital.

The Sunday meal was especially good during one of Ann's visits. Roast beef, mashed potatoes and gravy. Heaps of fresh bread, garden salad, plenty of cold milk and a slice of apple pie. We ate slowly, savoring every bite. We were chatting with some of the staff when I was paged by the operator. There was a new admission and I was needed for the intake evaluation.

New cases usually required quite a lengthy work-up, but the rest of the afternoon's schedule was rather light, so Ann decided to rest in my private room until I'd finished. It proved to be a fascinating problem and I was so wrapped up in the burdens of the unfortunate man with *dementia praecox*, that I was gone for several hours.

Ann had napped and then decided to take a long, lingering tub bath. She filled the tub nearly full, locked the door, afraid that someone might wander in, and enjoyed the luxury of the hot water. She heard me enter the room and promised to be right out. I listened as the water swooshed down the drain. Then a long silence. Finally, an embarrassed half-whisper . . . "I'm stuck. I'm stuck in the tub. I can't grab onto the sides enough to get out."

I rattled the door knob. "Honey, it's locked on your side. There's no way I can get in to help you."

There was a little panic in her voice.

"What will I do? I can't stay here. Maybe you'll have to take the hinges off or something so you can get in."

"The hinges are on the other side, too. I'll have to get the janitor. He might be able to figure something out."

"Don't you dare! I don't want any stranger gaping at me, thinking I look like a beached whale."

"How about the window over the tub? Think I could fit through there? I can get a ladder and it'll reach the window. Thank heavens we're on the first floor."

"It'll be a tight fit but I'll bet you can do it. I wish you'd rush."

If I had spent many months in the Psychiatry rotation and had all those fancy meals, I wouldn't have been able to slide through the window. But the space was just large enough for me to crawl through and free my very pregnant wife from her awkward imprisonment.

CHAPTER 4

✍

Becoming a Baby Doctor

The clinching argument for pediatrics came when our son, Frank, was five weeks old. The early days of his life had been rocky, but he had become more interested in his feedings and was gaining weight at last. Ann was exhausted by the schedule of 10-2-6-10-2-6 feedings and when I'd come home from the hospital clinics, I'd find her uncomplaining but completely fatigued.

It seemed that giving Frank his bottle shouldn't be too much of a trick and so I suggested that she get some sleep and I'd see to it that he took his formula. Ann agreed to let me manage our son's feeding and went off to bed, after placing him properly in my arms and tucking his bib securely under his chin.

The rocking chair was a little small for me, but I thought that I could stand it for twenty or thirty minutes and began with confidence. He started off beautifully, pulling on the nipple eagerly and seemed well on his way to emptying the bottle in jig-time.

"Everything all right?" my wife's voice asked from the other room.

"Oh, sure," I replied. "G'wan to sleep. We're doing fine."

I watched the clock carefully and when ten minutes had gone by, I thought the time had come to burp the baby. I put him over my shoulder, gave him a few whacks, brought up a questionable bubble or two, and started to feed him once more. Somehow or other, I couldn't get him back in the position in which Ann had placed him. Neither the baby nor I was pleased with my body hold. During the manipulation, his bib fell to the floor, but after some contortions, I managed to reach into the dresser drawer and pull out a clean one. I fumbled for several minutes before the bib was placed again. At last everything was ready.

For some moments we proceeded wonderfully. Then my right foot fell asleep and I had to uncross my legs and try to find a comfortable position. Another nuisance was an itching sensation along my nose, just under the mask. I ignored it and went on with my task. But the itching

28

persisted. I couldn't stand it any longer. With the baby and bottle cradled in one arm, I reached under the mask with my free hand and massaged my nose.

Forty-five minutes had already gone by and Frank had taken but two ounces of milk. He had been burped twice and I had taken the bottle from his mouth five or six times to read the level of accomplishment.

The doctor in me knew from the textbooks that the whole feeding ritual should take but twenty or thirty minutes. The mothers in our clinics are told that a baby gets all he needs in the first eight minutes. But the father in me reasoned that Frank was small and needed his feedings, so I figured an exception could be made in his case.

I started to rotate the nipple in his mouth, hoping to stimulate the sucking reflex. I pleaded with him; even started to threaten him. Then I removed the bottle, rolled up my sleeve and tested the warmth on my skin. The milk was too cold. No wonder he didn't want it. Back it went into the warmer. Three ounces left. If Ann found out that much remained, she'd be heartbroken. Then a sudden fear hit me. Supposing the baby wouldn't take another drop. How could I explain it to her? For a moment I thought about drinking it myself.

The formula had been warmed sufficiently, I guessed, and again I tested it on my forearm. It seemed a little too warm, but it would have to do. A glance at the clock convinced me that I couldn't wait to have it cool down. Sixty-five minutes spent getting just two ounces of formula into my son.

I readjusted the bundle in my arms, uncrossed my legs again and reached for the bottle. The too-warm milk drizzled down into his stomach and promptly returned. One look at his regurgitation and I jumped to my feet, holding the baby firmly in my arms. "Ann, Ann," I yelled, quite horror-stricken she told me later. "Ann, could you please come here right away?"

She was startled into instant wakefulness and rushed into the nursery. I stood there with large beads of sweat on my forehead, breathing rapidly and completely done in.

The experience was humbling. Book learning be damned. I realized how little I knew. I applied for a residency program in Pediatrics and vowed to collect some practical skills along with the esoteric theories of child care. Throughout the years parents, grandparents and patients have taught me as much as my professors.

We gathered up the crib, playpen, stroller, favorite toys and a few other essentials and started our nomadic life. We joined in the hunt for knowledge and set up housekeeping in a one-bedroom apartment, six miles from the hospital. I had advanced to the senior residency in Pediatrics at a good training program in Westchester County. The salary was seventy-five dollars a month and we paid forty-eight dollars in rent and had the balance for food and incidental expenses.

Learning to take responsibility for the welfare of patients was a crucial part of my training. A number of foster children were placed under my medical supervision. I was obligated to visit them at home whenever they were ill. My territory was the entire county and as the hospital was in the center, some calls carried me twenty-five miles away from my base.

One of the messages that was stuffed into my box one day was a request to help Tooey. Two maiden ladies were caring for a pair of brothers and the older boy, seven year old Tooey, was having trouble "catching his breath." I drove the county car as fast as I dared and entered the world of the eccentric, elderly foster parents.

They escorted me through doily-studded rooms to where the boy was. Both women were solicitous about Tooey's condition and expressed hope that I would be able to give him relief.

"The people at welfare didn't tell us about his asthma," said one of the sisters. "It's a big job to feed and bathe these boys. We have to do their laundry and make sure they study. All that for the little they pay us."

"And then to make us worry when they're sick. It's not fair." The other sister scowled as she added her remarks. "Tooey, the bigger boy, is a lovely child, but what Lydia said is true. Doctor, it's a shame that we get next to nothing for the care we give."

Tooey didn't look too pleased to see them and he studied me with suspicion too. His breathing was labored and the respiratory wheezes were signals of his distress. There were several toys near him, which he clutched possessively.

The effort of breathing fatigued him and he needed the support of the rumpled pillow to remain upright. I noticed a crop of sores scattered over his chin and cheeks. I knew that these festers had been present for a considerable time since some were crusted over, while others were angry, oozing lesions.

I opened my medical bag and gave him a lollipop which he took with delight. Then I examined him carefully, trying hard not to exhaust him or arouse his hostility. When I had finished, I left the bedroom with the pathetic youngster still working hard to get air.

The sisters followed me down the circular stairs, past stained glass windows to the parlor. I sat down on one of the mohair chairs and looked at the two ladies. They were fidgeting, nervously, with the collection of china birds on the coffee table in front of them.

I was anxious to get back to Tooey but needed some background about his symptoms. The scene that had just taken place had modified my opinion of the women. There was something disarming about their high-collared dresses and prune-wrinkled faces. It was almost irreverent to suspect that their sweetness and musty charm could conceal their negligence as proxy parents for Tooey.

Finally, I said, "Miss Miller, this boy's asthma is severe. He's not in any danger right now, but he could change at any time. It started because he's highly allergic to something. It's not the pollen season, so we'll have to look somewhere else. Now, what kind of pillow is he using?"

"Why, feather, naturally."

"Is the mattress horse hair?"

"I imagine it is, Doctor."

"Has the house been painted lately, either inside or out?"

"Not is the last two years. We meant to have some done this year, but prices have been too dear."

At this point the younger brother ran into the room. He was hustled out by one of the sisters immediately.

"How many times have you been told to stay out of this parlor?" she said as she forced the frightened child through the door. "These children are very difficult to train, Doctor. I'm at my wit's end sometimes, trying to make them behave."

I said nothing. In the fleeting glimpse I had of the boy, I noticed the same sores on his hands and face that his brother, Tooey, had displayed.

I continued my questioning.

"Are there any pets in the house?"

"Why, yes, Doctor. We have a dog. A French poodle. Her name is Marie. We've had her for five years. She's beautiful."

"Do the children play with her?"

"Oh, no. They're not allowed in this room or in our study. We keep Marie in there most of the time, except in the evening when my sister and I sit in here. We sew or listen to the radio and we let her stay with us."

"I see. Well, that's probably the cause of Tooey's allergy. And if he has more contact with the dog, he'll have more attacks. I'm afraid there's only one thing to be done. The poodle will have to go or he'll never be free of asthma."

The sisters stared at me in amazement. Then one spoke up.

"Doctor, you're wrong. Not Marie. The boy will have to go."

There are times when you wish a glance was more graphic. That you could express contempt with a lingering look. But I picked up my kit and walked upstairs without a word. I dressed the asthmatic child as well as I could, wrapped a blanket around him and carried him down the stairs. The sisters were waiting in the hallway.

"I'm talking Tooey to the hospital with me," I said. "The social worker will be here this afternoon for the other child and she'll return your blanket."

As I left the house, I wondered how many other myths would explode as I visited more homes and saw more of disease. It was so hard for me to think that a child was less prized than a pet. When I discussed the event with one of the more experienced doctors the next day, he consoled me. My anger was not surprising, he admitted, but there was a lesson for me. I had to stop being judgmental. The sisters had different values from mine. They were sputtering, he guessed, about the high-handed way that I had behaved when I carried Tooey from their home. The social workers must have gotten an earful that afternoon.

The next part of my training took place in Chicago. That's when I became aware of the effect of poverty on the health of patients. Many of the families relied on our outpatient services for their medical needs. My clientele lived under deplorable conditions for the most part. Crowding, inadequate heating, rodent-infested flats accounted for many hurried trips to the hospital.

. We treated burns, rat bites, sometimes lead poisoning: all direct results of environmental hazards. The poorer families learned that car battery cases were an extra heat source during the winter months. They would pick the dumps clean of the discarded batteries and when the temperature fell, they'd toss the cases in with the logs. High levels of lead would be released in the fumes. Having inhaled the fumes, a convulsing child not infrequently ended up brain damaged.

The emergency room handled such problems around the clock. I had to answer them many nights after a full day of caring for the hospitalized patients. It was not unusual to have the benches as crowded in the late night as during they day.

I was asked to see a five year old late one night. He was quite composed as the nurse finished taking his temperature, pulse and blood pressure.

"He's all yours, Doctor," she said. "He's got a runny nose. Not much more that I can see." She patted him lightly. "Take it easy, Reggie. The doctor won't hurt you."

I asked Reggie's mother what was bothering him.

She hovered protectively over him.

"He's here because of the pneumonia."

"The pneumonia?"

I looked at Reggie. Nothing very threatening about his breathing. There was no hoarseness, no cough. No surprises in the rest of the exam either. A little redness of his throat and eardrum. Lungs were crystal clear.

He winced when I touched his abdomen, however. The smile left his face and he gestured to his mother.

She pushed me aside, lifted Reggie off the table and yelled for the nurse. "Where's the bathroom? Hurry up. He can't wait!"

Reggie returned a few minutes later.

"You see, Doctor," she said, "you've got to take care of the pneumonia."

It might have been my lack of sleep or the early hour, but Reggie didn't seem to be at high risk.

"There's no pneumonia, Ma'am," I said with confidence. "All I can find is a little head cold. Really, that's no emergency. You could have waited until morning to call."

Again Reggie cried out and clutched his middle. He was shuttled to the bathroom and back once more.

"Doctor," she repeated, "take care of the pneumonia."

"You keep saying that. It seems as though he's having more trouble in his gut. Those trips across the hall."

"Exactly. He's been like that all night. Child with a miserable cold going out in the snow every time he gets those cramps . . . we ain't got no plumbing at our place. You mean to tell me he wouldn't have pneumonia by morning if I didn't bring him here?"

I had to agree. A child with diarrhea in Chicago in the middle of winter. I could imagine the wind blowing off Lake Michigan and Reggie's rush to the outhouse through the snow drifts. We were able to find a bed for him and put his mother's worries to rest.

Those years in the hospital clinics and wards annealed my mind. There was an imprint that was not erasable. For the rest of my life, I would have to be an advocate for children. The price would be constant availability. The reward—watching a generation or more grow.

There was a detour along the way. My commission as a Lieutenant (jg) in the Navy came, as well as orders to report for active duty. I had a brief indoctrination at Great Lakes Naval Station and was then assigned to sea duty.

A pediatrician on an attack transport. Not a very useful pairing. It didn't appear that my training would be helpful aboard ship, but it promised to be an unforgettable adventure. I reported to my post in San Francisco and was told that my ship was anchored in the bay. After a short wait, I boarded a small boat and was taken to the side of the *USS Chilton*. It loomed several stories high as I readied myself to climb aboard. The waves lapped against the side of the ship, rocking it gently.

The boat crew of the small craft watched as a Jacob's ladder was lowered down the side of the *Chilton*.

"That's how you get up there, sir," one of the men said. "Here's your gear." He handed me my suitcase and steadied the rope ladder as the bottom flapped against the ship.

I started my climb. "Forget your gear," yelled the coxswain. "We'll send it up in the cargo net later."

The deck crew urged me on as I timidly inched my way up.

Why couldn't the bay have been calm, I wondered? Helluva way to have an officer who is afraid of heights report for duty. How many more feet to the top? Steady. Steady, I reminded myself. It's easy as long as you don't look down.

I faced the deck officer. "Lt. Roberts reporting for duty. Request permission to come aboard."

"Permission granted."

They showed me to my quarters and I stowed away my things. As expected, my tour of duty was filled with excitement. There were new illnesses to study. Our ship's sick bay was packed with men from combat zones with malaria and other tropical diseases that challenged our skills. The badly wounded personnel were cared for on the hospital ships but we found enough casualties to keep us hopping. Every now and then a sailor would test my pediatric knowledge with a case of scarlet fever or the mumps, but most of our time was spent treating gonorrhea or some exotic skin rash.

One unlucky sailor complained of severe abdominal pain while we were at sea. The weather was foul. We had skirted the edge of a typhoon and the ship bucked and rolled as we were hit by the storm. It was hard to know who was more frightened as the waves tossed the *Chilton* about, the patient or me. We strapped him to the operating table and I performed the only appendectomy of my career.

There is an old Navy tradition. The crew has to be kept busy, even when in port. The bos'n's whistle would send the men to their work stations and the maintenance on the ship would begin. Invariably, the chipping hammers would start pecking away at the rust on the steel decks as I was listening to someone's heart in sick bay, one deck below their clatter. It seemed to me they painted and repainted the deck over my head a dozen times while I was on the *Chilton*. In a way, it was good training for civilian life. After all, I would need to filter out the deafening chorus of babies' screams when the war was over.

Overseas duty gave me a taste of the hell so many servicemen face. Years later the clang, clang sound of imminent danger would awaken me from sleep. I would be startled with the chilling words, "All hands man your battle stations." It was a shared, bitter memory . . . a warning that a kamikaze pilot was headed toward our ship . . . that our convoy was under attack . . . that there was an enemy force at hand. Those dreams were so vivid that I'd jump out of bed and start for my post at the forward part of the *Chilton*, then slip back into grateful realization that it was a haunting return to past terror.

There were visions of children caught in the web of war too. The shortage of food made the young victims as desperate as the other noncombatants. We'd watch dozens of them swim beside the ship when we'd tie up in port. We'd throw coins over the side and cheer as the young divers captured them almost in flight. Enough to buy the family's meal at the black market. When we went ashore, there were pot-bellied, hungry children with their hands out, begging for some of our abundance. They asked for chocolate, for pennies, for cigarettes to trade for food.

In one Chinese city we saw a couple carrying a blind, deformed child. His arms dangled flaccidly at his side. One foot was clubbed. My friends and I pressed most of our change into the father's hand and left as quickly as we could. What future could that child have?

A few weeks later we made another liberty stop about fifty miles from the last one. We hailed some rickshaw runners and were carried from the dock to the town square. A familiar couple approached us as we left the rickshaws.

"Cumshaw, Joe? Cumshaw?"

The man grinned toothlessly. The woman turned the blind, helpless child towards us. We again felt their need and offered them a few more dollars. Their portable, handicapped child was their only source of income.

I thought, Dear God, where do we begin? So many who need help. I hope that I never forget children like these.

My friends and I wandered through the teeming streets. There were stores of every description with fine silks and jade and silver jewelry. The press of the crowds in this provincial city was overwhelming. In the markets we watched the women shop for produce, picking through the skimpy supplies for the best purchases. In one section huge, silver fish were weighed on a primitive scale. Then a piece of string was tied around the middle of the fish and it was handed to the housewife. She dragged it behind her in the dirt as she went from stall to stall until her shopping was done.

We went back to the pier to wait for our return boat ride. None of us had much to say. The beggars and the poverty of the people left us with a feeling of despair, and we had only seen the outer crust of this alien land.

CHAPTER 5

∽

What Can Happen To a Baby?

My stint in the Navy was over. It was time to support my family as a pediatrician. No better place to begin than my home town. There would be a nucleus of friends and some hospital contacts from my earlier days in training to help launch my career.

We looked for suitable office space and finally found a group of rooms that could be used. There was enough footage for a waiting room, consultation and examining room, and a small laboratory. The location was acceptable; on the second floor of a building with another doctor and a dentist as tenant neighbors. Young parents didn't need a building with an elevator, I reasoned, and the rent would be easier to manage without an imposing lobby and facade as prestige builders.

Ann and I furnished the area with the necessary essentials, filling in with second-hand waiting room furniture and hand-me-down lamps and drapes until our budget was exhausted. Then we waited for the flood of patients to begin. I had met the deadline for listing in the current phone directory when I opened my doors, but I wasn't besieged with calls. I had followed the usual courtesy and visited the older, established pediatricians and offered to take their night calls whenever they needed some respite. Medical ethics permitted the publication of a small announcement with an identifying photo in the newspaper and it was also in good taste to send fliers to the doctors in the community telling them my practice was starting.

Our nights were quiet. There was no demand for my services and we passed our time with old friends, strengthening social ties that had been halted during my years in training and the time in the Navy. One young woman was expecting her first baby. She was an effervescent sort who chattered endlessly with Ann about the wonders of the pregnant state. She had no apprehensions about the remaining months of her pregnancy nor of the delivery itself. Her confidence about the utter normalcy of child rearing was so great that she turned to her husband and said, "I've made up my mind. Fred will be our doctor. He's new at it. But after all, what can happen to a baby? Yes, let's make him our doctor."

There was no stampede of others with similar daring, willing to have a novice assume charge of their children's health care. Fortunately, some of the obstetricians took note of my empty schedule and recommended my services.

The first newborn assigned to me was in some difficulty at birth. He was a full-term baby who didn't pink up as promptly as most do and was quite sluggish when handled or fed. The nurses were worried and called me many times during the week he was in the nursery. I was convinced that he would be normal and managed to transfer my optimism to the parents. The grandparents would have preferred a grizzled veteran but did not voice objections to the young mother. (In later years my grey hair and receding hairline upset some that I might not be modern enough to handle their needs.)

I scheduled an office visit for one month after the baby's discharge. To insure an air of bustling activity, my wife and our two young children arrived in my waiting room a half-hour before the first fee-for-service patient arrived. I called my family in and we visited for awhile. When they left I reminded them loudly that their next appointment would be in three months and was grateful that the children played it straight.

The infant had thrived since leaving the hospital. He was a sturdy, pink-cheeked boy with a lusty cry. He had a shock of coal-black hair and deep blue eyes. There was a suggestion of a double chin already. All worry about a sluggish start for this robust boy had disappeared. The beaming father asked for his bill for my hospital services and after searching for a few seconds, I produced it. He handed me a fifty dollar bill.

It had never occurred to me that I might have to make change. My cash drawer was empty. But I couldn't let this first fee get away. I asked them to dress the baby and wait in my consultation room. I raced down the stairs to the gas station on the corner, got the fifty changed, then turned and bounded back up the steps to the young parents' side. The transaction was completed. The twenty dollars entered into my ledger was the only income recorded for my beginning week of practice.

Gradually my practice grew. There was no need to stock the waiting room with my own children. I was able to think of hiring a nurse when an offer came to join another doctor who had been ill and needed an associate. His case load was enormous, and I soon found that I had time for nothing but work. My mother's predictions had come true. I'd sit at the table, drinking coffee and munching on a sweet roll, when the phone would ring. I'd be out the back door and on my way to a patient's home, never finishing my snack. Ann became reconciled to my lifestyle and brought our children up nearly alone.

When I look back at those years, I realize that thousands of babies have been entrusted to my care. Most of them are a blur on my professional landscape. Their talents, their gifts, their lovely features failed to make a lasting impression on me. They needed no help. I was merely a witness as they passed through the stages of their childhood.

But the others . . . they line up in my memory. Many of them were guarded by their parents with fierce devotion, as if tenderness alone could compensate for twists of fate. Others were abandoned by family and society and found no champions. I could not explain why one parent would donate an organ for his child, while another would batter a two-year-old senseless.

There were happy endings to most of our cases . . . if it had been otherwise, I don't think I could have continued.

Rusty, for instance, was a three-year-old boy with headaches. Not a common complaint at that age. His father was still in the Navy, so Rusty had medical care, but there was no continuity to it, with all the moving about from duty station to duty station.

His uncle, a Jesuit priest, brought him to the office. He had been a chaplain for the local National Guard unit and knew my partner. The senior member of our practice was on vacation and I had to substitute. Our office was packed with a double load of children when Rusty was ushered in as a work-in.

When I saw him I forgot about the bulging waiting room. Something very unusual was happening to this little boy. He couldn't tolerate the overhead lights and sat upright, his eyes squinched shut. He had been getting worse, according to his uncle, for the last several weeks. Every morning he'd stumble to the bathroom, throw up and return to bed. He'd pull the covers over his head and try to sleep. The headache would lessen and he'd try to find an interest in play, but the pounding pain would return and he'd run to his mother and beg for help.

There were some soft signs on the neurological examination. I found a change in his reflexes and a little unsteadiness to his gait. A look at his eyegrounds showed blurring of the optic discs.

We needed a neurosurgeon in this case, so I buzzed my secretary.

"See if you can get Dr. Carter on the phone. If it's his day off, leave a message to have him call me tonight."

I told Rusty's mother and his uncle that further studies were needed. Then I spelled out the various possibilities.

Rusty went through the tests and underwent surgery before the week was out. Doctor Carter found a growth, an astrocytoma of the cerebellum. He was able to remove it completely and Rusty rejoined his father at Great Lakes Naval Station. The tumor was benign. The kindest words in the dictionary.

Making house calls in the northeast in the middle of winter is risky. But that's where we saw most sick patients during the early years of practice, so the weather had to be battled. The chains of my old Pontiac gripped the snow effectively. During one of those winter nights, I backed out of the driveway and headed out into the storm, after scraping enough ice off the windshield so that I could peek at the highway. There didn't seem to be much glamour in a profession where every night on call was spent behind the wheel of a car. But I couldn't stall for a more convenient time. Peter's bellyache was getting worse. I had to see him. The appendix could perforate in a matter of hours and his history was suspicious.

Not much traffic at 2 a.m. I parked in front of the small colonial-style house. The porch light outlined a narrow path to the steps but the snow continued to fall, cancelling my footprints almost as soon as they were carved on the sidewalk.

"Poor Peter," I thought. "It takes my hands forever to warm up in the winter. He'll hit the ceiling when I examine him."

The family congregated around Peter. He was on the living room couch, doubled over in pain. It was a typical story. Tender right lower quadrant, rebound discomfort and muscle guarding. A routine textbook case of acute appendicitis. They were wise to call when they did.

But I was distracted from Peter's difficulties. There was a strange-looking figure who was peering over the bars of a crib. The bedroom door was open and she was able to watch all the action from a perfect vantage point. I tried to get her attention but she ignored me and rocked up and down, making the springs squeak in harmony with her excited giggles.

Peter's father came close and said, "Please do something for Peter. He's having an awful lot of pain."

"Sorry. I'll make the arrangements now."

I called the nursing supervisor, the surgeon and my answering service, and we were en route to the hospital. Peter sat, wrapped in a warm robe, in the back seat of my car; his mother beside him and his father driving close behind.

The brief look that I had of the child in the crib upset me. She was a cretin. Once you had seen someone with the characteristic features, it was hard to forget. But the mystery was, who was she? My partner and I had taken care of Peter since his birth. No notes about any other children. Was she part of their family? I'd have to wait until we took care of the sick boy before my question could be answered.

The surgery was quick and Peter was running around the hospital wards within a few days. The time was right to talk about the little person in the bedroom. Both parents were hesitant but finally told me that she was their daughter, three years older than Peter.

"Now that you know, Doctor, don't let them take her away," her father said. "She's different. Anyone can see that. But we love her and don't want her to be taken from us. No institution . . . do you understand?"

"Nobody will do that. But maybe I can help out in another way. Why don't you let me see her. I'll come to your house."

He shook his head. "We don't need help. Thanks anyway. We can manage. We always have. Our family sticks together."

"There's nothing to be afraid of," I persisted. "You won't lose her. I promise. She'll stay with you. But sometimes we can make big changes in her kind of condition. It can't hurt to try, can it?"

He looked toward his wife. "What do you think, Sally?" Then he turned back to me without waiting for her answer.

"She's been scared that it was her fault. You know . . . that Doreen's like that. Doreen was born after Sally fell down a flight of stairs. When she saw how the baby was, she didn't even let her folks handle her. First grandchild on both sides. Wouldn't let anyone take care of her. Only herself."

He was quiet and then asked, "Are you trying to tell us that the fall had nothin' to do with how Doreen is?"

"I'm positive. I'd like to prove it with some blood tests. They'll show her thyroid gland isn't working. Then we'll start her on some tablets . . . you know . . . to make her grow."

They told me that Doreen was ten years old. She had no teeth. The soft spot was still open wide. Her features were coarse and her brittle hair extended down her forehead. Her face was puffy and her hands were broad with short fingers. She was the size of a ten-month-old baby. No speech at all and little expression to her face. Sometimes she giggled, I remembered. Her thick, protruding tongue made her sound stuffy all the time.

The medicine worked and Doreen's appearance improved. After several months, a more delicate-looking young person was able to be propped upright in a chair. By stages, development of teeth, closing of the soft spot and growth in size excited her family.

The delay in finding Doreen made greater gains impossible, but when she finally walked and managed some words, there was cause for celebration.

What can happen to a baby? Indeed. Thinking about the lawsuit and the interaction between patients and their physicians set the thought wheel spinning again. This time with more images of the past, of other days and other cases. Out of my inventory of nearly-forgotten events, the recollection of Maria and Nick's experience reconstructs itself in my mind.

Maria sat at the kitchen table. She sorted and folded the laundry. Frilly dresses, blue jeans, white dress shirts for school, men's work clothes. She looked up when Nick came in.

"Give me a hand, will you? Get the ironing board out and we'll have coffee while I get going on this. It's easier when I have company."

"Sure enough. I can use the lift. Gotta work late tonight."

Maria walked to the stove, turned on the burner and started the kettle. She spooned out two portions of coffee, found some Danish in the breadbox and started back to the table.

"I wish you didn't have to work again. The kids miss you. This'll be the third time this week you've had overtime."

"Honey, I'm lucky to have a job. They're layin' people off all over the place. I hear they're going to close down the color TV section at GE. Movin' out of town. They'll be gone by Christmas."

"I know, Nick. Even so, we'd like to have you with us more."

She heard the kettle's whistle and said, "This'll be my third cup today. I ought to cut down. Maybe that's why I get heartburn."

They were silent while they heard the rare quiet of the morning. She looked up at the clock.

"I'd better finish the ironing. They'll be through with their naps pretty soon. If I put it off any longer it'll never get done."

She stood up and reached for the basket of clothes. She touched the iron with her testing finger and began her chore.

Nick watched her quick movements. The way she worked fascinated him. His shirts were soon ready and on a hanger. Everything so organized.

She stopped suddenly and put down the iron. Her color was strange. Maria hurried toward the bathroom and he could hear retching sounds and then the rush of water.

Moments later she came out. Pasty and exhausted, she motioned to him to put the laundry away.

"What's happening, Maria? What's the trouble? You look terrible. C'mon, lie down."

He steered her into the parlor and held her hand as she sagged onto the sofa, like a deflated beach ball.

"Nicky, you'd better get to work. I'll be all right. It wasn't the coffee. It must be number eight's on the way."

He clasped her tightly. "That's what it is, huh? Well, well . . . number eight. My God!"

"Are you mad?"

"Mad? Of course not. They're pretty close together, but we'll manage. My folks did. And so did yours."

He caressed her gently. "Better see the doctor. Just to make sure. Call today."

"I will. It's a waste of time, though. I'm never late unless I'm pregnant, Nicky. You know that."

She looked up toward the winding staircase. A pair of faces stared between the spindles. Two sturdy children in sleepers, one holding a battered teddy bear, the other a blanket, waiting for permission to dash towards their parents.

Nick perched each on a knee, tousled their hair and said, "How about going to Gramma's? I think she's baking cookies and might need some help. We'll surprise her. Okay?"

He dressed his excited young ones, then he said to Maria, "Call the doctor today. See if he can check you while the kids are at your mother's."

He raised his hand and blunted her protest.

Maria's pregnancy was different this time. Her energy and patience were tested. Waves of morning sickness drained her strength and her blood pressure climbed alarmingly. Her ankles swelled and her weight soared. The obstetrician advised her to stay off her feet as much as she could. It made medical sense but there was no one else to fill her place. The only time she could rest was when the older children were in school. Then she'd cuddle the two young ones beside her in bed for a brief nap.

She managed somehow and was delivered at full term. Both mother and baby did beautifully and Maria was discharged to rejoin her family. When she entered the house she was greeted by her friends and relatives and her children lined up, waiting to view their new sister.

Cookies and fruit baskets covered the dining room table. Maria sat, unbothered by the bedlam all about her, while Nick presided over the homecoming celebration. He poured more wine for everyone and offered another tribute to his wife. Then he picked the baby up and strutted around the room accepting the admiration of his guests. When his triumphant tour was completed, he carried his newborn to her bassinet in the nursery.

Maria watched her well-wishers leave and sent the older children back to school. Nick cleared the dishes, put the packages of new baby clothes in the closet, kissed Maria and started for work. The house was quiet. It was time for the nap that had become tradition during the months before delivery. She herded the little ones into her room and fell asleep within minutes.

When she awakened, her two-year-old was crying. She had not had time to pay attention to her and knew how much she must have been missed. Maria swept the child up in her arms and showered her with kisses.

"Baby was hungry, Mommy. She was crying. I fed her. Okay?"

Maria raced to the nursery. Her baby was still and silent, two large grapes pressed into her throat.

When I heard the news I hurried to their home and joined the dozens of people trying to offer words of consolation. Nick and Maria accepted their well-meant sympathy but seemed to be out of reach to everyone. They listened to the priest and recited the familiar prayers of their faith and then seemed locked in their private grief.

After the others had gone, I sat beside the young parents. My primary goal was to remove Maria's sense of guilt. The awful accident was unavoidable, of course, and there was no way it could have been anticipated. I thought of the young sister and wanted to make sure that her innocent act didn't make her a pariah in the years to come. The chilling event was part of my learning process—understanding how to deal with death.

CHAPTER 6

✍

The Birds and Donald

I watched the birds build their nests in protected places at our summer cottage. Under eaves, guarded spots on our open porch, even the vent pipe of an abandoned heater . . . each place a target for their building wizardry. Once the nests were finished, the mating over, the mother birds flitted endlessly on their feeding flights. The growth demands of their newly-hatched young required the plucking of vast numbers of worms from the fertile country soil. Gradually, the birds grew; the fragile chicks were ready to fly. The cycle was over and the nests were vacant.

Donald came to my office swaddled in several layers of clothes and blankets, carried by his sheltering mother while his father and grandmother formed a protective flank.

"This baby won't take a thing, Doctor," wailed his mother. "I tried to nurse him but he wouldn't suck at all. Then I used the formula the hospital suggested. He spit it up. Mom got some Carnation milk and Karo syrup. It worked on me, she said. Same thing. He threw it up. My friend's baby, just as old as Donald, he's taking goat's milk."

I tried to keep up with her rapid-fire recital.

"Slow down," I suggested. "Take it from the beginning. Tell me about your pregnancy. Were you well? Did you have any trouble with the delivery?"

She chuckled and pointed to her husband. "No. Not with me. But with him."

"That's a switch. What happened?"

"We wanted to do everything together. Donald's our first, you know. Those classes at the hospital. We went to all of them. The Lamaze course. Greg here, is a little afraid of needles . . . just like me . . . but he promised he'd be at the delivery. They're letting fathers do that at our hospital."

"Good idea, too," I said. "The few fathers I've talked to say it's an experience they wouldn't miss. Go on. I didn't mean to interrupt."

"We got rather excited when I started in labor. Greg called the doctor when the pains were every three to four minutes. We were told to head for the hospital. It was in the middle of the afternoon, during visiting hours. Greg let me off at the admitting office and went to park the car."

I wondered if I would be given a step-by-step account of her entire labor, but I said nothing.

"He couldn't find anywhere to park in the lot. He had to go to the garage up the next block. He ran back to the hospital, poor guy, but I was already in the delivery room. That's how fast I moved along. They prepped me in a hurry and called my OB man. Lucky for me, he was in the hospital."

"You went real quick for a first baby," I observed.

"That's where we ran into trouble," she said. "In class they discussed how the husband scrubbed, put on a gown and mask and stood at the head of the table in the delivery room. He was part of the team. He was supposed to hold her hand during labor pains and help her with her breathing and her contractions. When the baby came, the instructor said, the doctor would do a few things; clear the mouth, clamp the cord and so on, and then put the baby on the mom's tummy. That way, both of them would get a look at the same time"

Greg looked a little ill at ease. He added a few comments.

"Doctor, it's as she said. They'd taken her upstairs to be delivered by the time I got back. I had to wait for the damn elevator, it seemed like forever. Everybody was busy . . . rushing around . . . couple of the other women were close too. One of the nurses finally took pity on me. She showed me where to wash up, helped me get into that stupid outfit and led me to the delivery room."

"He walked in . . . didn't know where to go. My OB man let him stand at his side. The baby was coming. Greg saw all that blood, saw the baby's head and heard me cry out. That's all the remembers."

"He passed out?"

She answered for him. "He keeled over backwards and hit so hard that they had to call for someone to revive him. My doctor was busy with Donald and me."

"Quite an experience."

"That's not all. He got such a whack when he fainted that he fractured his skull and they kept him in the intensive care unit for four days. As a matter of fact, the baby and I went home before he did."

Greg piped in. "It was very embarrassing. And when I had to stay in bed at home for two weeks, I have to admit that Donnie's crying got to me. Geez, Doctor, they did everything to make that baby eat. Just to satisfy him so he'd quiet down."

"That's a new one. Maybe you've been a little impatient because of Greg's injury. I've learned that some babies can't get on schedule for a few months. But we've talked enough. I'd like to see how your son is doing. Then we'll discuss what to feed him."

They had reason to be concerned. At six weeks of age, Donald weighed less than birth weight. Sunken cheeks, skinny rear end, alert eyes.

"Did you bring along a bottle? Formula, water, anything? I want to watch him feed."

The baby drank the five ounces in no time. I watched him as he lay quietly on the table, now wearing just a diaper. He began to squirm. Then deep indentations were visible over his abdominal wall. He let out a cry and gobs of formula shot past my shoulder.

"See," the grandmother shouted. "He does that every time. No sooner does he finish, then he loses everything."

I felt the baby's now-relaxed stomach. There was a swelling, about the size of an olive, below the muscles of his abdomen.

"There's no trouble with the formula. Your son had a rather common condition, usually in boys, We call it pyloric stenosis."

"I think I read about it in the baby book," she said.

"You probably did. It's a narrowing of the far end of the stomach. Milk, water, nothing can get through. But don't get scared. If you read your book again, you'll find that a simple operation takes care of it. He'll be as good as new."

I arranged to have the baby admitted that day and advised Greg to stay at home . . . didn't offer to have him watch the surgery.

Donald doubled his weight in three months and ballooned up to thirty pounds by his first birthday. His near starvation before the pyloric stenosis surgery had made both parents focus on feeding past the point of reason. Every pound he added was welcomed, as though it would insulate him against future illnesses.

Every time I counseled them to cut back on his diet, they nodded but ignored my advice. He was a bright, passive child with legs as round as small tree trunks and piles of fat that oscillated every time he tried to run. He was a mountainous, timid child content to watch the other children climb the jungle gyms or try their skills as steeplejacks.

Greg tried to interest him in his ten-speed bike, enrolled him for karate lessons when he was eight years old, even begged Donnie to jog with him, but he met opposition from his wife and mother-in-law.

"You know his allergy is terrible. Didn't you hear him cough last night? Do you want him to collapse? He needs his rest. That's what he needs."

"Rest? That's all he does. The kids make fun of him, and I don't like it. The doctor can give him something for his asthma. But he's not gonna have a friend in the world if this goes on. Did you ever hear the names they call him?"

She answered, "Greg, there'll be time for all those sports later on. But for now I'm going to have an excuse written so he won't have to take gym. He gets all sweated up and then catches cold and ends up with bronchitis."

"You're making a sissy out of him. I'm telling you the other boys will never stop teasing him if you don't let him do anything."

"Over my dead body," she said stubbornly. "When he's older, but now let me decide what's best for him."

The battle went on. Greg found himself isolated from his son more and more. As for Donald, he was a frequent visitor to my office. Many times I could find little reason for the visit but the conversation followed a predictable pattern.

"Don't you think he's pale? Shouldn't we get a blood count? He's so tired all the time, Doctor. Maybe he needs vitamins."

"I doubt he needs vitamins. He gets enough in his diet. And I think you'll agree that Donald eats enough."

"Not really." She wasn't giving an inch. "He never touches a vegetable. I can't get that child to look at carrots . . . won't even taste a string bean or broccoli."

"Are their any foods that upset him?"

"Oh, yes. He breaks out from eggs . . . gets hives all over his body. Fish works the same way. Within minutes his lips will swell and he'll itch like mad. Let's see, chocolate, oranges, tomato sauce, peanut butter make him deathly sick."

"Hives from all of those?"

"Sometimes. But it's the asthma that's the worry. If he gets the slightest cold and has eaten some of those foods, he gets all filled up. I can't count the nights I've sat up with him, Doctor."

"There's allergy on both sides of the family, isn't there?"

"Not on my side. His father has hay fever and when he gets near cats he sneezes. But that's about it."

I listened carefully to his chest. "Donald sounds clear today. No congestion in his lungs and his temperature is normal. I'll check his blood but I'm not expecting any problems." Then I added, "We really ought to do skin tests to nail down his allergies. Can you make an appointment for an afternoon after school? Maybe next week?"

"He can come any time you say. I've kept him out of school this year because of his tiredness and coughing. They send his work home and Donald keeps up that way."

"Who writes his excuses? I know I haven't."

"I had a conference with the principal. He said he'd allow Donald to study at home as long as he kept his grades up. Greg and I had a terrible fight about it."

She stopped, started to cry and then went on.

"My husband doesn't understand that some parents let their children go to school half-dead. They must want them out of the house. Not me. Donald's my whole life."

"You can't wrap him in cotton batten," I said. "He should have contact with kids his own age. Don't worry so much about germs."

"I'm disappointed in you, Doctor. You must have forgotten how sick he was. Greg's the same way. You know he's moved out? He's been gone for the last six weeks and Donald's awfully upset."

I tried to calm her down. We agreed to do the allergy testing as soon as my work load allowed. I wasn't too surprised that Greg had left for his own apartment. He had stopped in to discuss the way his wife was babying Donnie and was ashamed that he had not been more assertive.

He told me there were weeks when Donald was a virtual prisoner in his room; thermostat set at 72 degrees; windows closed to avoid a draft. His meals were brought to his room. They even bought a portable refrigerator to store perishable snacks.

"Doctor," Greg said to me, "you've been taking care of Don since he was born. I know he's had a lot of trouble with asthma and all that. But, damn it, the guys at work have kids too. Some of them have been as sick as my boy. But they're not coddled forever."

I nodded. "Greg, some women can't forget the tough times. They want to shelter their children. I've seen it happen over and over."

"But it's getting worse all the time. Have you seen Donnie lately?"

"A few months ago. He's due to come in for his yearly exam soon.

Why do you ask?"

Greg let his head drop. He whispered like a conspirator.

"She's driving me nuts. I've talked until I was blue in the face. She coops him up in that bedroom. Brings him his homework and while he's studying, she makes him sandwiches and pours him glass after glass of milk."

"Sounds all right to me. But I wish he'd get some exercise. It would help his asthma . . . increase his breathing capacity."

"You won't believe this," Greg said. "Donald will be sixteen next month. He's going to graduate this year. Get this, Doctor. He will be the valedictorian of his class and he hasn't set foot in school in over two years."

"Incredible."

"Yes, it is. Never got involved in any school activities; no dates; no friends over to watch TV or listen to the stereo. Sits in that room, as I said, like a prisoner. The only difference is the way his mother feeds him."

He stopped, pulled a notebook from his pocket. He tore a page loose and put it on my desk. I scanned his entry.

"June 1st, weight 300 pounds. Up ten pounds since February. Finished a whole salami, one loaf of bread and a gallon of milk while studying for exams."

"Greg, you didn't write down how many days it took to eat and drink all that."

"One day! Doc, it's like that. No matter how I yell at her. She gives me that look. There's no way I can reach her. Please, I beg you. See what you can do. Three hundred pounds!"

It amazed me that there was an end to the forced feeding of the gigantic teenage. I would have bet anything that he would remain an elephantine recluse for the rest of his life. To my surprise he entered college on a scholarship and moved into the freshman dormitory. An influence stronger than mine or his father's lured him into a more normal eating pattern. I never met the girl who wrought the miracle. I'm glad she came along.

CHAPTER 7

❧

Bethany's Bump

My first afternoon appointment was with Bethany. Bethany bubbled into my office. A tall, pretty teenager who presented a common complaint: messy skin. She rattled on about other topics, reminding me to be sure to give her a signed health form for cheerleading and girls soccer. She hated to be examined at school, she told me. It was too fast. No privacy, really, and you couldn't ask the doctor some of the questions you'd been saving up.

I let her catch her breath and had my nurse get her ready for her physical. It was my policy to have a private interview with the patient and then have a chaperone join me for the examination itself.

"Anything special on your mind?" I asked when we were alone.

"A couple of things, Doctor." She looked worried and said. "My weight . . . it's gross, isn't it? Can you put me on a diet?"

"Let's see. At your age you should weigh one hundred pounds for five feet in height, and five pounds for each inch over five feet. So, one hundred fifteen pounds would be the average for someone five foot three inches. You are one hundred and twelve. Just right."

"I'm so fat, though. I'll have to take off a lot before school. My girlfriend's taller than I am, and do you know what she weighs? Ninety-eight pounds!"

"Bethany, let's go on to your other questions. We don't quite see eye to eye on the diets."

"My periods. They've been real bad. Got anything for that? It's mostly my first day."

"We can work something out. There are some new drugs that are good for the cramps. I'll write you a prescription when we're done."

"That'll be great. Here's what really bugs me. These pimples. I look as though I've got terminal acne. It'll probably leave scars that will never go away."

"Anything else?"

52

"The pill. Do you think I should take it? It might help my skin."

I rang for the nurse. Then I said to Bethany, "I'll try to answer your questions one at a time. Let me do the exam and then we'll talk."

She was relaxed as I began my inspection. The nurse recorded the normal findings on the office record. Healthy kid, I thought . . . at the prime of her life. A touch of dandruff. Certainly not from neglect. She was like the rest of them, shampooing every night. The acne wasn't very bad either. Some on the forehead and around the chin. A few on her back. They dramatize every little item at this age. I felt for glands in her neck and had her swallow to check the thyroid region. All in order . . . except the firm lump on her face, just below the cheekbone, might need to be watched.

I finished the rest of my testing and found no other worries, but I couldn't help feeling a gnawing concern.

"All done," I said. "Is your mother in the waiting room? I know you don't need her with you. Not at your age. But I thought we might chat a little. The three of us. Do you mind?"

Bethany got down from the table. She didn't seem to sense that I had much to say. Might preach some about her diet but she knew I wouldn't betray confidences.

"Mom's out there. We've got to stop at the record store for new tapes for my stereo."

The nurse left the three of us. I reviewed all the normal findings and handed Bethany the permission slip for sports.

"You're all set," I said. "I'll give you some samples that you can try for your menstrual cramps. If they help, I'll phone the pharmacy for some more. By the way, did either of you ever notice that round bump on Bethany's left cheek. It's about as big as a marble. Do you know what I'm talking about?"

Bethany's hand shot up to her face. She hunted around and then paused.

"Mom, he means this. It's been there a while. I thought it was one of the zits."

Her mother touched the spot.

"That's new as far as I can tell. Bethany would be able to figure out how long it's been there. She spends half of her life in front of the mirror."

"Why don't I see you next week? I'd like to check it again. It may be gone by then—if not, it's still a few weeks before school. We can take care of it.

They were leaving, not knowing that the small ball didn't belong there. A list of possible causes flashed through my mind. Cat scratch disease was a candidate; a cyst in one of the oil glands . . . or a tumor.

"Bethany," I asked hopefully as they were leaving, "do you have a cat?"

"No, Doctor. I'd love to have one but Mom is allergic to them."

The bump was a mite larger when Bethany came back the following week. It had to be biopsied. She was no frothy adolescent now. The acne shriveled in importance. To her credit, she kept her composure in spite of the burning doubts in her mind.

"This biopsy," she asked, "will there be much of a scar? I mean, will I be able to cover it up?"

I assured her that it would scarcely show.

"The plastic surgeon I've asked to do it is a wizard. And, Bethany, you will be home the same day. They've got an arrangement. It's called in and out surgery; it cheats you out of visitors. You won't be there long enough to get any cards."

The trip to the hospital was quick. A few stitches and a bandaid handled the wound. The hard part was the wait for the report of the specimen of her bump. Bethany plunged into the new semester with her usual intensity. Clothes, books, sports and boys distracted her preoccupation with matters of health.

The lesion was malignant. An insidious kind of growth that sent out tentacles and had the capacity to invade the nearby tissues and spread through the blood stream to other parts of the body.

The choices had to be presented to Bethany and her parents. This part of pediatrics was unenviable. My awareness of this malignancy's potential had to be outlined without crushing her spirit. I couldn't recite statistics—those unfeeling numbers that gave her less than a ten percent chance to survive. Nor could I paper over the gravity of what she faced.

Bethany's decision when she learned about her options was instantaneous. She voted for life. She cried as hard and long as anyone when she heard that she would need major surgery, followed by a long course of chemotherapy. The operation would mutilate that side of her face and she would need a series of later cosmetic repairs—if—if they could remove the entire tumor and destroy its seeds with the anti-cancer drugs.

Bethany's treatment took a whole year. She submitted to all the pain and tolerated the loneliness with a kind of courage I had never seen before. The cancer specialists sent me lengthy reports and Bethany's file was crammed with details of surgical techniques and reactions to radiation and drugs. Little was written about her emotional equilibrium. Had it been shredded by the march of events since I first discovered the little growth in her cheek?

She was anxious to catch up on everything that had happened during that lost part of her life. She had been discharged to my care and I was to monitor her recovery with bi-weekly examinations. Bethany would be with a new class in school. This peer group would be younger, but she'd be back in a culture with a focus on rock music, dates, fast cars, college aptitude tests and the entire adolescent whirl. Her new friends would still have that wonderful feeling of immortality. Maybe she could climb aboard again.

CHAPTER 8

෨

Donna and Her Boys

Some medical discoveries arrived too late to rescue my patients from age-old plagues. Other critically ill people were saved by the blessings of the antibiotics that cascaded from the laboratories in ever-increasing numbers. For the millions who would recover the typhoid fever, syphilis, tuberculosis, meningitis, pneumonia and countless other scourges, we could delight that we were conquerors. But what about those who were lost before the remedy was found? The joy in the triumph of disease control is blunted by thoughts of what might have been.

Paul and Donna taught at the high school my children attended. They were the parents of three red-headed boys, and they chose me as their pediatrician. On several occasions I was asked to stop by their rambling house on a sick call. They lived at the top of one of the hilliest streets in town and twenty or more concrete steps carried a visitor from the street to their door. Most of the time I looked forward to the summons. It was an interesting home, filled with antiques and a glow of living. A baby grand piano was at one end of the huge living room and comfortable chairs and a long sofa allowed their guests a chance to lean back and enjoy their oldest boy's virtuoso performance of the classics. He played the way my mother dreamed I would. The fireplace was flanked by floor to ceiling bookcases and I was certain that every volume had been read, probably more than once.

Most of my calls were to treat a case of laryngitis or a sky-high fever. Usually it was an acute problem with a simple solution. I'd rummage through my bag and often find some medication to carry through the night and then would sit and unwind in front of the fire. Our friendship grew during those early years and it was an effort to interrupt the flow of conversation and head for my next stop.

Paul called me at the office one spring afternoon and asked me to look in on Donna when I made hospital rounds. She was in the gynecology section, one floor above the pediatric wards. I promised I'd stop by. He didn't offer any background details. Just thanked me and hung up.

I had visited with Donna after each of her deliveries and commented that I was making a social call this time. She put me at ease right away. No long face or catch in her voice. She held out a box of candy and said, "From my sons . . . they just left. Of course they had to try out each row, but there's still a pretty good choice."

I selected a chocolate peanut cluster and munched away.

"I'm glad they missed this one," I said.

"That's my favorite kind, too. But they've got me on a liquid diet now. Another reason for me to be mad at that damned tumor of mine."

She went on. "It took me by surprise. The tumor, I mean. It's a pretty wild variety. By the time you realize something is wrong, it's had a head start." She stopped and looked hopefully at me. "Can you sit awhile? I haven't seen you in months."

I perched myself at the foot of the bed. "I don't have anybody waiting to see me. I'd love to keep you company if you're not too tired."

"Paul and I have talked this over," she said. "We've gone over all the options. They boil down to more surgery with no real chance of recovery or this . . ."

She pointed to a bottle suspended on the bedside pole.

"The oncologist was honest with me. He said I could count on some more time if I opted for their new drug; it's experimental. It may slow down my kind of tumor."

"I've read about good results in children with solid tumors. Some have been in remission for three or four years. A good remission, Donna, where they can't find the growth, as though it's been checked."

She shook her head.

"He didn't give me that kind of hope. Not with this type. Maybe an extra four or five months to be with these guys." She pointed to the picture on her nightstand.

Her red-headed twin boys, her husband and their gangling thirteen-year-old son were smiling broadly.

"I'm proud of that pose," she said. "I took it with an old brownie camera we had for years. I've had it blown up, and it goes wherever I go."

"Donna, I remember when you had the twins," I said studying the faces in the photo. "You were still living on the farm, weren't you?"

She smiled at the mention of the dairy farm.

"We had wonderful times there. Paul used to get up at the crack of dawn to milk the cows. Then he'd drive to school. Lot's of work, Fred, but we were dirt poor, barely squeezing by, and his salary wasn't much then."

"You moved into town when the twins were born, didn't you?"

"We had to. They needed a lot of care. I couldn't do much and still be with them and there was no way we could afford help. So we had to let the farm go."

"The twins are about ten, aren't they?"

"Yes. Just had their birthday. We had a break with the farm, though. When we sold it, we cleared enough so that we were able to make a nice down payment on our house."

"It sounds as though you still miss the farm."

"Sure. But it worked out for the best. Paul stuck to teaching and he's vice principal now. Little Paul hated it when we moved to the city, though. Scarcely talked to us for weeks. He's got the heart of a country boy, I guess. That kid knew every flower, every tree that grew. He caught frogs, picked berries, even helped his dad with the milking. Wasn't the same for the twins. And when they started kindergarten, I went back to school with them. Of course you know that I've been teaching music in the upper grades for the last couple of years . . . until now."

"Donna," I said, "I'm here because Paul asked me to stop and see you. I knew you were going to a gynecologist. You told me that last winter when I saw one of the kids."

"That when they found the cancer. Adenocarcinoma of the ovary. They opened me up, saw what a mess there was and closed me right up."

I winced. Donna was self-controlled as she told me about the malignancy. Straight-out statements, no self-deception.

"Did they start you on chemotherapy then?"

"X-ray and chemo. It wasn't doing much so they suggested this experimental stuff. But the reason I wanted to see you was for advice about the children."

"Do your boys know how sick you are?"

"Not yet. They know I've had to get treatments at the hospital but not much more. That's my question. How much do you think they should be told now?"

I looked at the wasted face of my friend and searched for the best answer.

"I've always thought you and Paul were very wise in the way you brought up your boys," I began. "We used to talk a lot when I'd make a house call."

She smiled. "We did, didn't we? Paul and I would pin you down and fire away with our questions."

"Yeah. The minute I'd come in, you'd put the coffee pot on. And after I'd figured out what was wrong with the patient, we'd compare notes about everything under the sun; when to send them to nursery school, camp, discipline and all that. If I remember, I was permissive; you and Paul were tough. We didn't always agree, but we sure went on and on."

She tapped me on the shoulder. "You're dodging," she remarked. "Help me decide on the best approach now, not think about the old times."

"All right. My feeling is that you have to let them know now. If things are as bad as you say they are, ease them into it slowly. Children are surprising in what they can handle if they're given a chance."

"We agree for a change. The best time to tell the boys will be when they let me go home . . . later this week, I think. There's a rest period between courses of chemo. I'll be with them for a few weeks before I have to come back for another round.

"I've been lying in bed, thinking about young Paul. The twins, they're busy with so many things; they're not the kind to worry. But the big one is different. He's a brooder. He doesn't let anyone get near him. I hope I can be around long enough to help him cope."

It was a very busy spring for my practice. The usual cases of bronchitis and a load of children with middle ear infections claimed my attention.

Donna called to tell me that she had let her children know that her time might be limited. They had smothered her with attention and had behaved beautifully towards each other . . . as if they could reverse the sentence by their good deeds. Young Paul hugged her and promised he'd help keep his brothers in line. He reminded her how grown up he was.

She confided in me that she was slipping. She couldn't stand the sight of food and much of what she did eat, she lost. The doctors told her that she'd have to spend more time in the hospital for parenteral nutrition, as well as the cancer therapy. They conceded weekends at home.

Naturally I was depressed when I finished our conversation. Donna was irreplaceable. Those years with her family were bound to leave an imprint; a path for them to follow. I felt certain that this special woman's influence wouldn't vanish with her death.

In early July, Donna requested a house call. Her children had some vague symptoms and she was apologetic.

"Ordinarily I wouldn't bother you, Fred. I'd handle it myself but I'm home on a pass and I get worried if anything's wrong."

"I'll be glad to stop by," I said. "It'll be about an hour, though. Is that all right? I have to see someone in the hospital first."

"Don't rush. Paul's not here yet. There's a teachers' meeting but he'll be done by the time you get here."

Paul, the eldest son, was lying on the sofa. Andy and Jack, the twins, were in the bedroom. I started with Paul.

The city was experiencing its usual summer anxiety. The fear of polio had caused some of the beaches to be closed and nobody wanted to be in crowds. The newspapers added to the hysteria by reporting the number of new cases on the front page each day. Although Donna hadn't mentioned it, I knew she was in equal dread of a polio outbreak.

I flexed Paul's neck and noticed how stiff it was. He couldn't sit without help and then had to support his back in a tripod position. The most ominous sign was his difficulty in swallowing. Bulbar polio . . . no other infection likely. I went into the bedroom to see his brothers without sharing my findings with his parents.

Andy and Jack were not so involved. But both had suggestive neck symptoms, low grade fever and complained their muscles hurt.

We rode to the hospital and over the next few hours confirmed the diagnosis on all three boys. Poliomyelitis. No magic treatment for this disease. We could sit back and wait with the twins. They were not at immediate risk, but Paul's bulbar involvement was progressing rapidly. He was put in a Drinker respirator when his breathing muscles failed.

All Donna could do was watch as her son was kept alive in the "iron lung." She sat in her wheelchair as we tried to sustain him. When Paul closed his eyes for a short rest, she was taken to the twins' ward. The entire wing of the hospital was set aside for poliomyelitis patients. The nurses fished hot, moist woolen blankets from the row of washtubs that lined the hallways and applied them to the affected limbs of the paralyzed patients. The Sister Kenny treatment was in wide use for those whose skeletal muscles were involved, but there was no remedy for the type of damage that threatened Paul.

Donna sat near her son through his rapid downhill course. He would awaken briefly, smile at his parents, then slip into a quiet sleep. His body was encased in the device that breathed for him; only his head and neck remained outside. The sound of the machine filled the room and both parents stayed with their son until his death. Their cries were unheard until the respirator was disconnected.

When young Paul died, Donna was taken back to her room in the nearby hospital. The intravenous feedings were started again to keep her going until she could watch her son be put to rest.

The twins were not paralyzed and Donna was able to spend each day with them until they were discharged. She did not survive long enough to receive another weekend pass.

I never forgot that family. The Drinker respirators were stored in some warehouse, and the khaki army blankets for the Kenny treatment became relics of a futile past, once vaccines to prevent poliomyelitis were discovered. If only immunization against infantile paralysis had been available ten years earlier . . . if only.

CHAPTER 9

❧

Vinnie and the Red-Hot Appendix

Most of my days followed a pattern. Hospital rounds in the morning, then a home visit or two before office hours. Office hours were unpredictable, usually packed with minor complaints perceived as catastrophic events by anxious young mothers. This one spit up the formula, that one had a diaper rash or was teething. Scarcely testing grounds for what a pediatrician was supposed to know.

But sandwiched in with the routine were puzzlers; an occasional heart-stopping emergency, a baby who stopped breathing, another one with convulsions or a screaming child with a strangulated hernia. My pulse would speed up, and the urgency of such matters would erase the scheduled agenda from my mind. The pile-up in the waiting room placed great pressure on my office staff, but they were able to pacify most of the impatient mob with a smile and such lines as, "The doctor would do the same if it were your baby," or "You can't stick to the clock when you're a pediatrician."

My lunch break was often spent at a nearby diner, owned by Vinnie. This interesting fellow ran a place that specialized in quick snacks at the counter or wolfed down at one of the oil-cloth-covered tables. His main interest was not in meatballs or delicatessen but in the gambling room behind the shuttered doors of the luncheonette. That's where he took bets on horses, football games, numbers; even a menu of craps or blackjack.

Vinnie usually sat with his back to the wall, telephones within easy reach, so he could control the many phases of his operation. Most of the time his face was impassive and he would stare silently for minutes, shifting a big cud of tobacco from side to side before speaking.

It was a different world in that room. No diners in there, but serious men watching the turn of the cards and scowling as piles of money moved from one to the other.

"Doc, you don't want to be back here," Vinnie said the first time I went searching for a phone. "Nothing here to interest you."

"Of course not, Vinnie, just have to call the office so they'll know where to reach me."

"Take this phone then. The others are for business. Then, why don't you have Josie fix you up with lunch. And, Doc, I know how busy you are. Relax. You can use the phone any time you come in."

Vinnie's six children were included in my roster of patients. He was a blustering, bossy parent but attuned to every sniffle or scratch. There were four girls and two boys in the family. Each was indulged by this gruff parent, but the youngest son, John, occupied a special place in his life. Vinnie treated him as heir apparent to his kingdom.

Vinnie tapped me on the shoulder during one of my speedy lunch visits. He rotated his tobacco cud more vigorously than usual and pointed to the back room.

"Doc, my wife's on the line. See what you think. It sounds to me that my Johnnie's real sick. But she's been with him all day; let her tell you."

I listened to Carmella's description of the boy's symptoms and agreed that he should be looked at. No sense in going back to the office. I headed out to Vinnie's house, a few miles outside the city limits. It was set on top of a hill, flanked by tall poplar trees with large gardens on either side and a full-sized swimming pool in the middle of the huge backyard.

I parked my car behind Carmella's Cadillac convertible and waited for Vinnie. He pulled me along to the front door, bellowed to his wife that we had arrived and dashed upstairs to see his son. I followed at a slower pace and then went into the patient's bedroom.

Vinnie and Carmella watched every move I made. Johnnie cried out when I felt his abdomen. His illness had begun the night before and he had gotten more and more uncomfortable as the day progressed. Another case of appendicitis. They seemed to occur in bunches. He was the third child in a month who needed surgery.

Vinnie blanched when I told him what had to be done. He paced up and down, cursed a few times and then said, "Are you sure, Doc? Maybe it's just an upset stomach. You know how kids are. Maybe you can give him something. Don't they freeze the goddamn thing sometimes?"

"It's appendicitis all right. He'll have to be operated on, Vinnie. No other choice. It might perforate. We can't take a chance."

"No other way, huh? Will you do the cutting, Doc?"

"I don't do any surgery, Vinnie. We'll get someone who specializes. Just does surgery."

"You'll go along with him, won't you? I trust you. I don't know about the other guy."

"Vinnie, you don't need me. Besides I've got an office full of patients. They'll kill me if I don't get back soon. Don't worry. Johnnie'll be in good hands."

There was menace in Vinnie's glance and his voice.

"You go along with my son. I want you to watch that surgeon. I've heard about them. They take out the appendix. Then if it doesn't look bad enough, they rough it up with a piece of gauze or something."

He stopped, looked over at Johnnie and Carmella and delivered an ultimatum.

"Doc, we're friends. But get this. We're talking about my son. You be there . . . understand? I want you to bring me that appendix when they're done operating."

Vinnie was good at intimidating people, but I was accustomed to giving orders when it came to patient care. I smiled and stood my ground.

"I can't do it. The specimen will go to the pathologist. He'll study it and give his report. I'll save you a copy."

Vinnie was all for calling an ambulance for the hospital ride. Instead, he and Carmella went in Vinnie's limousine with their ailing son.

I was able to catch one of the pediatric surgeons between cases. He felt Johnnie's tender belly and agreed with the diagnosis. Vinnie stood beside the stretcher, a sullen guardian, waiting for the orderlies to wheel Johnnie to the operating room.

"Carm and I will wait for you in the lounge, Doc. Stick around."

There were no glitches. The surgeon worked swiftly and the appendix was ready for the tissue committee's review. A large, swollen, not quite ready to rupture organ.

Vinnie was pacing up and down in the visitor's lounge. He had abandoned his plug of chewing tobacco and was filling the air with cigar smoke instead. Carmella was thumbing through the pages of a fashion magazine.

"He'll be down to the recovery room in a few minutes," I announced. "He's fine. Nothing went wrong. The doctor will tell you about the red-hot appendix and then I can go to my office."

A smile crossed Vinnie's face. "Great. Now I won't have to use this." He patted a bulge on his chest wall and drew out a shiny revolver.

"For God's sake, Vinnie, why did you bring that thing with you." I cringed as he fondled the weapon. "Put it away, will you? Scares the hell out of me." Then I added, "They issued me a .45 when I was in the Navy. Everyone had to carry them. Even the medics. Mine stayed strapped to my side. I never fired it . . . not even once."

"Don't worry, Doc," said a relaxed Vinnie. "It wasn't gonna be for you. But if anything had gone wrong . . . if that surgeon screwed up."

Vinnie brought his son to my office several weeks later. Johnnie was all right but he needed a check-up before he started sports again. Vinnie handed me an envelope with full payment for my part of Johnnie's care and a fifty dollar tip. He was puzzled when I refused the bonus; the only one I'd ever been offered. He didn't realize that it couldn't soften the blow of what might have been.

CHAPTER 10

৶

A Spotted Communion

At the start of a new century the imprints of the past still served as historical markers. We read about the Black Death and other horrors and knew the graves of antiquity were filled with countless victims. Those memories have been compared to the present threat of AIDS on human survival. During the early stages of my practice there were enough minor epidemics to keep me busy, but the public wasn't terrorized. The one exception was polio, which frightened everyone. The common contagious diseases of childhood were troublesome nuisances and, I learned, made some people act in strange ways.

It was not unusual to have hundreds of children in a community need attention simultaneously when the "old-fashioned" or "hard" measles struck. There wasn't much we could do after verifying the diagnosis. There were characteristic symptoms to tip us off; runny nose, red, watery eyes and high fever. Strong indicators the child was coming down with the measles.

We could lessen the impact for unaffected contacts with a shot of gamma globulin. The child, so protected, might have a few of the annoying symptoms, as well as a slight rash, but would be spared nine days of a more serious illness.

The mother of one of my patients asked me to make a call one spring evening. Her seven-year-old daughter had been coughing the typical cough that occurs with the measles. It is a dry, unrelenting, tiring cough. She had fever and her eyes were weepy and inflamed. The clincher was studding the mucous membrane inside her cheeks. There, with my flashlight's beam, I could see sand-like white dots. Koplik's spots, found only in this childhood disease, commonly a day or so before the blotchy skin rash appears.

"Another case to report," I thought. Then I turned toward the parents.

"She should be up and around within a week. If she has any trouble—you know, fever stays up or her cough gets worse—just call me.

Most kids sail right through."

Her parents received my information with little comment. Then her mother surprised me.

"The measles . . . not just a bad cold? All right, we'll keep her in bed as you want us to . . . right after she makes her First Communion."

I was startled. "I don't think you understood what I said. She'll be covered with a rash and coughing up a storm. And that fever won't go away for a few more days."

The mother sat on her daughter's bed. She hugged her and then explained.

"Dawn's worked very hard getting ready for tomorrow's services. And you should see how beautiful she looks in her dress. Pretty as a picture."

I cut her short. "Really, you can't let this child be with the rest of the congregation. She's at her most contagious stage right now. Coughing germs at everyone. Besides, they'll send her home as soon as they see her rash."

A defiant father joined the discussion. "I've got to go along with my wife. She's right. Dawn's waited for this day for such a long time. Why, it might be another year before she can take part again."

He added another argument. "We're having seventy people over after church. To celebrate. Lots of them are out-of-town relatives. We're having it catered, and it's too late to cancel. What in the world would we do with all that food?"

He walked me to the door, thanked me for coming and promised they'd call if she wasn't better.

"She'll be all right. Maybe they won't notice the rash because of the veil. We can't break her heart."

What a dilemma! In fairness I couldn't report Dawn's measles until the spots were visible on her skin. By then she would be in a crowded church with her classmates. The ceremony would go on.

At least there would be no mystery two weeks down the line when a bunch of seven-year-olds started to cough.

CHAPTER 11

❧

Nanette

She was holding her Cabbage Patch dolls when I came in.

"What are their names?" I asked. "Esmeralda or Danielle or something like that?"

"Oh, no. This one's Lillian Marie and her sister is Phyllis Diane."

"That's nice." I sat down next to Nanette. "Some dolls have the silliest names, don't they?" I said. "But I want to talk about something else."

"Sure." She went through the ceremony of putting the funny-looking creatures in their crib, covering them up and reassuring them she would be back shortly. It amazed me how maternal a child could act at such a young age. Instinct or imitation of her own mother?

"I'll bet you're excited that your baby brother will be home soon. You'll be a big help with him, won't you?"

She agreed. "I'll get his bottle and tell Mommy when he's wet. And I'll get to hold him when he's bigger, too."

"I know you and your Daddy do a lot of things together, and, of course, you're busy with nursery school. Maybe you'll learn some new songs that your brother will like."

I stared at the little blonde child, unable to shatter her world. She sat on the table, unruffled by her visit; no tears in anticipation of being examined, no fear of being stuck with a needle. I turned and left the room.

"What did she say? Did she understand? I didn't her her cry." My secretary asked me, "Should I go in and be with her?"

"No. Not yet. I couldn't find the words. She doesn't know."

"What are you going to do? She's got to be told, poor thing."

"Of course she does. But the words choked in my throat. It will have to come from her father. Just as I thought in the first place."

Nanette waited in my private office for her grandmother. She had wanted to ask about her baby brother. But it was her mother whom she missed and nobody said a word about her.

I walked slowly down the hall with Nanette's grandmother. This time she wasn't filling my ears with reminiscences of how her children used to act when they were young. She held on to me for support.

"My head is spinning, Doctor. I don't know if it's from that sedative they gave me or what. I might have to take a cab home with Nanette. I can't think straight after all that's happened."

"No wonder. We'll get you a ride, but we'll have to finish with her."

"Yes, I'd better pull myself together. Forget about the taxi, Doctor. I have to keep my word with that child. I promised her a treat after we leave your office."

"Grandma," Nanette said, "can we go now? I didn't get a shot or anything. The doctor talked to me. That's all."

"Let's have lunch. We'll have our own party before the baby comes home. Just you and me."

"OK." Nanette jumped up and ran ahead to the waiting room. She put on a coat, hat and boots. She looked up at the receptionist, perched on a stool inside her glass cage. "We're going to lunch," she confided. "I have a new baby brother, you know, and I'll get to see him tomorrow."

Grandma followed after Nanette, dolls curled in her arms.

"Go back for your dollies' crib, will you, honey? I think it's in the doctor's office."

She leaned over and whispered to me. "Somebody will have to speak up. It can't be kept from that child much longer."

There was a catch in her voice as she reminded me, "Chris was my daughter. God knows I can't be the one."

They left my office together. The visit hadn't accomplished a thing. I slumped in my reclining chair in the library. Dealing with death was so hard. All of the responsible people in Nanette's life were trying to shield her. I was one of them.

That night I drove over to Nanette's home. Her father, Lenny, and I summoned enough courage to face the child with the truth. We skirted around what had happened with double talk until Lenny lifted his daughter up and embraced her.

"You'll have to me my helper, Nanette," he said, his voice steady. "Your Mommy's not coming home. She died, sweetheart. She died and she's with God. So you can see that I need you. I can't do it alone."

There was nothing I could add. I left the two of them, consoling each other. There certainly were gaps in my ability to help ease that kind of pain.

CHAPTER 12

⚬

The Politician

"I'm all mixed up. Can I come in and talk to you?"

Diane's voice was muffled. Her eyes were probably rubbed russet-red and she must have used a box of tissue drying up her tears. This young mother was one of my grown-up babies. She was still a child in my eyes, but her tone let me know that nothing trivial was on her mind.

She whispered a "thank you" when I said that I'd wait for her after office hours. I hoped that she didn't need marital counseling. Clint, another former patient, had served in Vietnam and his experiences had left him brittle when crises occurred. He leaned heavily on his young bride in plotting the course of their marriage.

Their first child, Scott, was a superb little boy, and when he was born, it made Clint's re-entry into civilian life much easier.

"My whole life hasn't turned to shit," he told me. "The guys were spooking me about Agent Orange. I didn't dare think what might happen with Scott. But you know how he's turned out."

With the second pregnancy, Diane felt a little different. When she went to the obstetrician for her first prenatal exam, he ordered a sonogram and repeated the tests several weeks later because of some worrisome findings. He shared this information with both parents, telling them that the implantation was good but that the growing baby had enlarged brain ventricles. That, he explained, translated to hydrocephalus and a handicapped child. He stressed that the likelihood of a normal life for the fetus, if it survived, was in doubt. They were advised to consider terminating the pregnancy.

She sat across the desk from me. A tiny young woman, not yet showing her second pregnancy.

"Clint will be here soon, Doctor. I hope you won't mind that we're bothering you with our troubles. But we didn't know where else to turn."

I wondered, in this age of computers, if I could get a count of the number of freckles that studded her cheeks. In some strange way, freckles seemed to go along with flawless health, with country living, with milking cows and all the other cliches. I certainly hoped that they would have a charm to insure a happy marriage. So many couples weren't able to work things out these days.

Clint, out of breath, barreled into the consultation room.

"Hope I didn't keep you waiting, Doctor. The traffic was brutal. An accident on the expressway backed everybody up."

They were petitioning me, not for my help in cementing breaches in their union, but to assure them I would be their advocate throughout the pregnancy. And that I would not suggest an abortion.

"We know there might be troubles. Big troubles," Clint said. "But Diane and I want this baby. We think it would be wrong to give up. Don't forget they scared us the first time too."

Diane echoed her husband's every sentiment. Their brave sounds may have been covering up their fears. But I agreed to call their obstetrician and arrange a consultation with the appropriate specialists likely to be needed after delivery. And finally, that I would be in attendance at birth.

The months before term were agonizingly long for everyone. Consultations were planned, as promised. The neurosurgeon would be on call to do a shunt if the collection of fluid continued to accumulate—fluid that could prevent the brain from expanding normally during the early months of life, if the pressure was not relieved.

Everything was set. The baby arrived about four weeks early. He had already been put in an incubator when I arrived. His color was poor, his respirations were labored and the large head, in proportion to his small body, made the diagnosis of hydrocephalus official.

His condition was precarious, and it looked as though this infant's life span would be brief. The respiratory distress worsened. His heartbeat was irregular. He was rather floppy and an early appearance of jaundice complicated his first days.

The neurosurgeon agreed reluctantly to follow the plan and placed the promised shunt as soon as the baby was adjudged to be a fair surgical risk.

I consoled the parents as best I could. They had made a decision that was right for them even though the prognosis for survival seemed bleak. I had to caution them that the surgery was no guarantee that he would develop normally.

The operation was done, and after a battle with feeding and more respiratory complications, he rallied enough to be discharged from the nursery unit. He went home at three weeks of life.

Clint buttonholed me at the hospital while Diane was dressing the baby.

"We haven't talked lately, Doctor," he said. "Diane says you tell her everything. But you look worried all the time. Are you holding something back?"

"No. I've tried to share everything with you. There isn't much to cheer about though. If you want to know, I'm concerned you might be getting your hopes too high because he got through a few tough situations. This business with the apnea monitor . . . "

He interrupted me. "We'll get used to it. They put them on a lot of preemies. We've talked to some parents who've had babies like Kenny. It gives them a feeling of security to have an alarm go off when the baby's not breathing. You can bring him around with CPR. Diane and I have been taught how to do it."

"It's a big responsibility. Having a monitor can make you uptight. You hope you won't be in such a deep sleep that you miss the beep."

"We know what can happen. Everyone has warned us. Doc, there's no one who hasn't been kind and caring around here. The nurses are terrific, and all those specialists are as good as you said they'd be."

He looked at his approaching wife and baby.

"We've plenty of faith," he went on. "Both of us. Listen, we can't get this far and give up on him."

"Good attitude, Clint. As long as you know the odds, I won't say anymore. We'll take it as it comes."

In spite of the upbeat talk, the first office visit was not encouraging. He looked like the runtiest runt of a litter. Scrawny legs and arms, an outsized head with eyes that squinted. Potbelly, pouting out, unrestrained by his weak abdominal muscles. They disconnected the leads to the apnea monitor and placed him tenderly on the scale. He seemed lost in the blue receiving blanket. He had gained but a few ounces since leaving the hospital.

Succeeding months were glum also. But slowly he put on weight and to our delight started to respond to the world about him. He smiled, babbled, regarded his parents as best he could with his crossed eyes. Several severe respiratory infections didn't do him in; neither did a bout of diarrhea. There was a celebration when they shipped the apnea monitor back to the hospital.

By his first birthday, he was a playful, functioning child. Another operation was necessary to correct hernias and undescended testicles. I shook my head in amazement at the way he grasped things. He had closed the gap in every way except size. It was strange to hear such a tiny child rattle off full sentences and recite nursery rhymes flawlessly.

Kenny learned to exploit his privileged position. His older brother and all the relatives lavished him with love and attention. He became a benevolent despot, ready to extend his rule. I had no doubt that he would charm his teachers and even his stronger peers.

When he was ready for kindergarten, his parents arranged for his required school physical exam. The talkative child was very much at home in my office. Our whole staff had watched over the years as he was piloted through the medical maze of tests and special education programs, through batteries of psychological studies and speech, hearing and physiotherapy classes. This was merely another of the nuisances, just another examination.

He stood on the scale, pulling himself up as straight as he could. Every inch was vital to him. The nurse pushed the ruler down gently. Barely three feet tall and all of thirty-four pounds.

He jumped off the platform, took his mother's hand and headed down the hall. My door was open and I watched him come toward me. His walk was jerky. He moved like an animated toy, stopping along the way to inspect our wall posters and to wave greetings to everyone in view.

He tilted his head to one side when he reached my consultation room. His eyes loomed impressively behind his glasses.

"C'mon," he said to his mother. "My doctor is waiting."

Diane picked up my willing patient and placed him on the examining table.

"Would you believe it?" she said. "It's time for his kindergarten exam. He starts school next month."

Kenny hurried his words. "I'll go on the bus with my brother. We'll have lunch in school with the kids. Mom says I can have money for milk, too. Just like Scott."

He was too big to cry when it came time for his booster shot. The ceremony was over. I filled out the health form and gave it to Kenny.

"You keep it, Mom," he said, as he climbed down. "Let's go. See you later, Doc."

CHAPTER 13

❧

The Office Party

Angie loved pasta. You needed only one look to know that eating was her favorite pastime. She tried to conceal her tremendous bulk with slacks and loose fitting blouses. Much of her time was spent in the kitchen, preparing and tasting traditional foods.

When her three daughters were younger, she took pride in their round cheeks and chubby bodies. It was cute and no one snickered then, when they passed. But to teenage girls who plodded like Clydesdales, obesity was a curse. The prospect of attracting a young man diminished with every added pound.

Angie's daughters longed for some medical magic that would allow them to compete with their peers. They studied the glamor magazines and envisioned themselves in high-styled outfits. They dreamed that someday they would walk down the aisle clothed like bridal models. They fantasized selecting filmy negligees for their trousseaus and bikinis that highlighted their slender young figures. Sadly, the more likely garments would be items from a mail order catalog in durable denim or sailcloth.

They begged me for diets and an exercise program to keep their weight under control Every morning the young sisters put on their jogging clothes and punished their bodies for three grueling miles. No matter what the weather was, the ordeal continued, slow-paced running that made their muscles ache and their knees swell. Their after-school schedule was strenuous as well. They competed with each other for the greatest distance registered on the exercycle. Some nights, Josephine, the youngest, was too tired to study and would fall asleep at her desk. Angie would mutter to herself and lead her to bed. The next morning, when the alarm went off, Josephine would jump up and join her sisters for the morning run.

They weren't successful at trimming down. Their muscles were firmer and much of the flab shrunk, but they still shook their heads in disgust when they weighed in at my office. Angie took me aside at one of the diet review sessions and gave vent to her disapproval.

"Doctor, you know these girls are being foolish. They've been on this nutty diet for weeks. They go out in all kinds of weather. Get sweated up. They're too tired to do a thing around the house to help me. And look at them. Wasting away."

I tried to keep a straight face. "Angie," I said, "I wouldn't use the words 'wasting away.' Here are their numbers: Lucy, 182 lbs; Rosa, nearly as much, 180½; and your little Josephine, 169."

I showed her the growth charts. Her daughters were way above the highest percentiles.

She was not impressed.

"A person has to have a little something to fall back on. In case she gets sick. They don't eat anything anymore. 'Too fattening, Ma. Too many calories.' That's all I hear. It drives me crazy."

Josephine gave her mother's theories a chance to be tested. She continued her daily work-outs and kept on her Spartan diet. She managed to lose a few more pounds, enough to give her some encouragement. When she developed a cough and low-grade fever, she insisted that she still had to run her three miles and do the stint on the bicycle. Angie's pleas were ignored. Josephine was going to be a size 12 or less, no matter what.

She fainted in school one morning. The nurse called her mother and reported that Josephine was having chills and that her temperature was over 103 degrees. The cough was worse and she had a "catch" in her side.

Angie called me that afternoon. When I examined Josephine, she really looked a wreck. Her right lung was filled with rales and she went into paroxysms of coughing when I asked her to take a deep breath.

"Old-fashioned pneumonia, Angie. Probably will have to be in bed all of this week. But she'll do fine. She's a strong girl. We'll start her on penicillin and give her some cough medicine so she can get some rest. And please keep her diet light until the fever's down."

"Pneumonia's not so bad, you say? It scares me. I remember when my grandfather had it. He was sick all winter."

"That was before antibiotics, Angie. Now it's cured in no time."

I wrote out the prescriptions. "Stop your worrying," I said. "Just get these filled and I'll be back tomorrow to see how she's doing."

Josephine was sitting on a chaise lounge on the sun porch when I made my next call. There was a tray at her side with an unfinished sandwich and a barely-tasted bowl of a thick soup. She seemed brighter, however. Her fever was lower and she had slept well.

Angie tucked the covers around her a little tighter, plumped up her pillows, refilled the pitcher with juice. She pointed to the dishes and told me confidently, "Once we get some good food into her, she'll be a different girl. You'll see. No more talk about calories. No wonder she was as weak as a kitten. These kids."

Whether it was the penicillin or the nursing care or both would be hard to judge. I saw her at home once more, then sent her back to school after her chest x-ray showed total clearing of the pneumonia. Angie was relieved to have her daughter well again. She felt that her recovery was due to the nourishing meals Josephine was forced to accept and to my medical advice. Every week she'd sew one dollar onto a letter and mail it to me to pay her bill. Money came hard since her husband's death. His pension was just enough to let them get by. She decided that there must be another way to show her gratitude for the extra attention she thought I gave her daughters.

Angie pulled her children away from the television set and steered them to the kitchen."Sit down and try my new recipe for apple pie. It won't kill you. I've been thinking we ought to do something nice for the doctor. Josie was so sick and he was over here every day. How about it?"

"Sure, Ma." There was unanimous agreement. "Something for his desk? Bookends? A Clock? Magazine subscription?"

Josephine volunteered. "Why not a scarf? Or a sweater? I could knit it for him."

Angie wasn't pleased. "My idea is better. Each of you can help and he will never forget this present."

Josephine ran to her room and slammed the door when she heard her mother's plan. She shouted it would embarrass her and she wanted no part of it. "A sweater would be perfect, Mom. Blue's his favorite color and I can find out his size from his secretary."

Angie prevailed. She conspired with my office staff to surprise me with a party at Christmas time. Everyone joined in the plot. I was told that this year we would have the meal catered, and I would have to get someone else to cover my practice that day. No excuses.

The table was set in our conference room. Everyone exchanged gifts, relaxed and sat back, sipping glasses of fine vintage wine. The door swung open and our cateress arrived. There was Angie, a few coarse hairs on her chin; globs of grease mingled with splashes of sauce on her clothes. A missing middle button on her white dress permitted some uncorseted fat to protrude. She bore a huge tureen and her daughters followed with bowls filled with salad and baskets of warm bread and pastries. She placed the steaming container on the table, donned an apron, piled spaghetti on the plates and clothed it with her special sauce. She chirped orders to her daughters.

"First the doctor. Then the nurses. Quick, Quick. While it's hot."

The girls went through their chores, still embarrassed by their mother, but anxious to please me. Angie glowed as we were served. It was a show of affection that touched each of us. She stood to one side, flanked by her daughters, watching our expressions.

We couldn't wait to start our banquet. But the gift that came from this warm woman was the worst meal that I had ever tasted. The pasta was glue-like and her homemade sauce defied description. How could she have spent so many hours in the kitchen, adding the choicest ingredients and end up with such a disaster? Somehow I managed to down my portion. The bread, baked elsewhere, was acceptable and I added another swallow or two of wine as an antidote. It took my finest diplomacy to refuse a second helping.

Fortunately, Angie did not realize that her art did not match her kindness. The next year we avoided another fiasco by eliminating our office party.

CHAPTER 14

❧

Cry Baby

"My baby hasn't stopped crying for the last two days. We're going crazy, Doctor. Come right away, please. I can't stand it much longer."

A call like that can't be ignored. The woman sounded desperate. Sometimes tragedies happen when a tired parent's quota of tolerance is expended. No need to risk a battered child.

"Let me copy down the address," I said. "I'll be over as soon as possible. Just finished office hours. In the meantime, a few questions."

I rattled off the usual inquiries. "Any fever? A rash? Any trouble breathing? Been feeding well? Been near anyone who's been sick?"

She answered no to everything.

It was only a short drive from my office. I pulled into the driveway and went around to the back entrance. The family lived on the third floor rear. It was a sweltering July afternoon. Some of the neighbors were preparing their barbecues and two teenaged boys were throwing a baseball lazily back and forth. Monstrous black flies were attacking a partly open trash container near the back door steps. I wished I had left my jacket in the car. It was too hot to keep up a formal appearance. I was sure that they wouldn't think any the less of me if I shed my tie as well.

I was about to ring the doorbell when I noticed that the boy's father was sitting in the backyard, stripped to the waist. He held a beer can in one hand and his fiddle and bow in the other. The lawn was cluttered with dandelions, almost obscured by the ankle-deep grass. His scraggly red beard and uncombed hair shrouded his face. He finally became aware of my presence and grunted a greeting.

"About time that she called you. Drove me the hell out of there. All that screaming. Nothin' we tried could get him to quit. Never heard anything like it."

He tucked his fiddle under his arm, threw the empty container in the waste bin and opened the door for me.

"It's up to the top of the stairs. Apartment 303. I'll be up in a few minutes."

I trudged up the dimly-lit stairway. Everybody wasn't cooking outdoors. There were penetrating smells of bacon grease from somebody's skillet at the first landing, mixed in with fish frying at the next level. Neither tempted my appetite on such a humid night. I hoped that my wife would have something a little lighter for me when I finished this call.

"Door's open. Come in. Excuse the way this place looks, but I haven't been able to do a thing. He just cries and cries."

She steered me past mounds of un-ironed clothes, piled high on the table in the small living room. We walked down the hallway to the kitchen. Dishes were stacked in disorder in the sink. A half-full nursing bottle sat on the counter with a bowl of cereal next to it, spoon stuck in the center and with a few cousins of the black flies from the yard buzzing about ominously.

The baby was thrashing about in his carriage. He was a bald, chubby child about ten months old. His face was contorted, as if he was in great pain. His entire body was flushed and drenched with sweat. The room had no ventilation other than a small expanding-type screen in the lower quarter of the window.

I placed my bag on the red metal table. The mother rocked the carriage back and forth, hoping to calm the baby. Then she lifted him out of the carriage and cleared a place in the sink.

"If you want to wash up, it'll have to be here," she said apologetically. "The bathroom's all plugged up. We called maintenance at least ten times, I'll bet. They said they'd be right over."

She handed me a bar of Fels-Naptha soap and some paper towels. By this time the red-bearded father had joined us. He found a sheet and put it on the kitchen table.

"Isn't there a bedroom . . . a crib for him?" I asked.

"Sure. But we can't keep him in it. He hates to be there even when he's well. So, when he's in the carriage we can quiet him some of the time."

The angular mother, a good head taller than her husband, put the noisy tyrant on the table. Her glasses kept slipping down her nose and she replaced them, all the while talking and soothing her child.

She reached into the pocket of her apron, fishing out a pacifier. Bending over the baby, she tried unsuccessfully to coax the rubber nipple between his lips. Her husband shook his head.

"He kept the whole building awake last night. They'll kick us out of this damn place if he doesn't stop his wailing."

I had them assist me as I searched for the cause of his misery. None of the reasons for this type of crying seemed to fit. Rectal temperature 99.6; no signs of injuries; no red ear drum to explain his fury; no trouble breathing. His heart rate was hurrying along with all of this commotion, but there were no murmurs or irregularities. I felt his abdomen. No muscle guarding; no masses that I could feel. Next, I took off his rubber pants and dripping wet diaper. Nothing to suspect that he had a hernia or a twisted intestine or the telescoping of one part of the intestine into the next . . . intussusception, that could give a story like this. It wasn't any of these. It looked as though we would come up empty.

The exhausted parents momentarily relaxed their grip on the baby. She sat near him and began to cry.

"We waited so long to have a baby . . . we certainly wanted him. But this is too much."

She reached for a tissue, dried her tears, and blew her ample nose.

"It couldn't be his teeth, could it, Doctor? We tried whiskey and teething lotion. Useless. The lady downstairs says that those bottom teeth are the worst."

"Not very likely. I usually save the mouth and throat for the last. It's the toughest part for the babies. They fight the tongue blade like a hooked marlin."

I positioned his father at the baby's head, instructed the mother how to restrain the legs.

"Teeth aren't coming in," I said. "But no wonder this poor kid's been so miserable these last couple of days. Take a look over my shoulder. I'll focus the light so you can see."

An open safety pin was imbedded in the right tonsil. I quickly traded places with the father, lowered the baby's head over the side of the table. With a hemostat I was able to grasp the pin and remove it. Rust had already started to show on the point.

"I'll be damned. A safety pin . . . a safety pin." The unsuspected reason for the baby's screaming had his father talking to himself. He wheeled the carriage over to the table and eased his son onto the mattress. "Maybe he can fall asleep now. Get his bottle, will you?"

Sometime solutions are simpler than they appear. Everyone knows that a child is inquisitive about the world around him. I'd have to include diapering in my list of home hazards when I instructed parents about accident prevention, along with coins, buttons and balloons.

CHAPTER 15

❧

The Golden Smile

"Zoe Pappas is calling," said my receptionist. "She wants you to stop over after office hours."

"Sure. Tell her it'll be late, though. We're waiting for that baby with convulsions and we have a college exam with the Wilcox boy at five o'clock."

"It's for her nephew. Zoe speaks better English, so she does the calling."

Miraculously, I finished at a decent time and called home with the usual news. Feed the kids and save something for me.

The Pappas family lived near my office. They ran a small grocery with a complete line of Greek imports. Their flat was over the store and the most wonderful cooking smells greeted me as I reached the top of the stairs.

Zoe answered my knock. A stout woman in her late forties, she was childless but occupied with the care of her three nephews. Her brother, Chris, and Athena, her sister-in-law, worked in the store from dawn until bedtime, trying to make a better life for the family. Zoe did the cooking and baking as well as a hundred and one other duties.

Zoe led me to the bedroom where Athena sat hunched near her son. She got up to greet me.

"She tell you," she said shyly. "No good like Zoe or Chris."

Alex had not been well for several weeks, I was told. First, a fever and some muscle aches. Then a sore throat and higher fever. His older brothers delivered his papers for him while he stayed in bed, so weak that he had to be helped to the bathroom. He couldn't shake his tiredness.

"Such a busy one before this," explained Zoe. "Running, running, running all the time."

Athena guided me to the bathroom. She opened a bar of scented soap, dropped the wrapper in the wastebasket and indicated that I should use the delicate guest towels after my hand-washing ritual. It took three of the tiny bits of cloth to dry my hands after the pre-exam scrub.

They left me alone with Alex. We bantered a bit before I started the physical. The walls of his room were covered with posters of his baseball heroes. Pennants of favorite teams as well as personal trophies and awards were close to his bed. I teased him about his Dodgers, mired in last place. He assured me that they would improve once they signed some new pitchers. The confidence of this thirteen-year-old in the future of his idols could not be shaken even though the season was half over and the sports writers had given up on the team.

My light-heartedness faded as I felt the walnut-sized glands in his neck, his armpits and groin. His liver and spleen were double their normal size and purplish bruises were visible everywhere. His color was waxen. Little doubt about what was wrong with Alex.

I told him that I'd leave some medicine to make him feel better and joined the family in the parlor.

"Zoe, can you get your brother from the store?" I asked. "Maybe he can close up early tonight. I want to talk to all of you about Alex."

"Sure, I'll go down." She patted Athena's arms, said something in Greek and left. The family sat in their parlor, reserved for visits from the priest, relatives from the old country and people like me. They seemed to shrink deeper into the overstuffed chairs as Chris and Zoe wrestled with the words that would explain to Athena that her son had leukemia.

We spent many hours over the next few months, trying to ease Alex's suffering and to prepare the family for the outcome. Alex never let us know about his terror. He accepted the countless blood counts, the transfusions, the long hospitalizations with grace. His parents were spared the pain of discussing the cause of his failing strength. He pretended that each drop of transfused blood made him better, that each new drug tried restored his energy. His deception gave some relief to his family. But Alex knew his illness was fatal. I had not withheld any facts when he asked how long he would live. I was vague about details but acknowledged there was no cure for leukemia. Patients were living longer and had remissions that were encouraging I told him. He thanked me for being open with him and we never discussed his future again.

When Alex died, Athena grieved in isolation. She shut herself away from friends and let her husband spend the long hours in the store without relief. Her despair heightened when she realized that her morning sickness and skipped periods were not the result of agonizing over Alex but the start of a new life in her forty-five-year-old body.

Her obstetrician proposed that a small amount of fluid be withdrawn from the sac surrounding the baby as abnormalities were more likely at her age. Athena waved the suggestion away. An abortion was unthinkable. She would care for the baby, whole or flawed.

When I looked at the little girl in the nursery, the perfection of her seven-pound body lifted my spirits. The new mother put her baby to her breast and wept as the drizzle of colostrum gave nourishment to this fresh life. Athena smiled at me and the flash of her gold teeth picked up the light streaming through the window.

Alex was not forgotten. But his room was not made a shrine either. His baseball memorabilia were stored in a chest in the attic. His clothes were given to the church and the trophies were placed on the mantelpiece in the living room. Chris and Athena talked about Alex as if her were still alive. He would always be a part of their family. The baby was a gift, not a replacement for their dead son.

Every month I looked forward to Athena's visit with Kristina. Zoe always came along with them. I had never seen an infant dressed so regally. Her pale pink dresses were hand-sewn and her diapers and undergarments were a dazzling white. They carried her to the examining table and placed an embroidered pillow beneath her head. The two women watched, enraptured by the squirming baby. They clucked and giggled when I weighed and measured the first daughter in nearly a generation.

Then Athena would dress her treasure, beam her special golden smile in my direction, and take Kristina home.

CHAPTER 16

❧

The Mother Who Wasn't There

The first time I met her in the hospital was during 1980, the later years of my practice. Molly was steeped in facts about the care of the newborn and asked questions about an endless variety of topics. "What's in the colostrum? What's that purple dye they've painted on my baby's cord? Why do they tell you to have your baby sleep on its stomach? Do I have to burp him after every ounce?"

I took twice as long to make rounds when she cornered me. I had to explain every hiccup and account for every ounce the baby lost during the first few days of life. She accepted nothing on faith alone. But when I noticed how quickly bonding took place between mother and child, I didn't begrudge the time. This woman, it was clear, was meant to have a flock of babies, and she probably would.

Her husband faded into the background. This was her show. He shook my hand, said he had heard a few nice things about me from some of his colleagues, excused himself and went back to his private island at the university. He was more at home in the chemistry lab with beakers and burettes than with diapers and feeding schedules.

During the first month or so that the baby was home, I answered all sorts of questions about diet and medicines. She wanted to make sure her breast milk was free of any foreign substances. Everything she ate was natural, grown without the aid of chemicals or adulterants . . . nothing with coloring or flavoring. Admirable motives, I agreed, but quite limiting in an urban community in the Northeast where the growing season was short and most produce had to be shipped from distant farmlands.

Her baby thrived. His only trouble was persistent constipation. She studied all the texts and wondered why her nursing infant didn't have an easier time with elimination. Breast-fed babies were supposed to have a huge advantage over formula-fed infants in this regard. She fussed with him, trying all kinds of tricks.

She brought him to the office in desperation, fretting over the irregularity of his stools. He was limp and lethargic. He refused to suck from her and choked on the bottle he was offered. His cry was a mere whimper and suddenly he stopped breathing for nearly half a minute. I grabbed an oxygen tank and held the mask to his face. He seemed to rally somewhat, and I began to piece together the history.

"How long has he been like this?" I asked her.

"Only since yesterday. I can't seem to get him to take anything. He's just blah. Scarcely moves."

"He won't nurse, I notice. Has he been taking much of the sugar water?"

"It's not sugar water, Doctor. I wouldn't give him that. My sister in San Diego sent me some pure honey. He'd take a little at first. I hoped it would cure his constipation, but he's no better."

I looked at the inactive baby. "We'll have to get him to the hospital. He'll need help with that muscle weakness. Not much I can do here. I'm sorry to tell you, but I think your son might be the first child I've seen with botulism."

"Impossible. Botulism comes from foods that aren't canned properly. I've read that there's a kind of toxin that can be deadly. Where could he get that?"

"From the honey," I said. "There are spores the babies get from some batches of honey. They aren't destroyed in the intestines and they make a poison. That may be what's making your baby so sick. But we'll talk some other time. Right now, we'd better get a move on. His color still isn't good."

The baby recovered. Molly was undaunted by her experience. She continued to read labels and be suspicious of established principles of child-rearing. She remained an enigma to me; different from the other mothers in my practice. We got to know each other, though, because Molly was fertile . . . pregnant nearly every year. She devoted all of her energy into caring for her children. She made their clothes; tutored them at home when she feuded with the school system over the curriculum; jogged with them; sang with them; tried to mold them into free-thinking souls.

When she paraded them into my office for their check-ups, bedlam would occur. Her young gang would rampage through my office like a tropical storm, turning over lamps, opening and closing drawers, switching lights off and on. She remained disconnected from their wild behavior, acting as if they belonged to someone else. She ignored her children as they dashed naked up and down the corridor, and when I tried to corral them in one room long enough to finish my examinations, she looked at me in a puzzled way.

"What can we do about the nuclear cloud?" she asked, as if we had been discussing the age of the atom all along, instead of the activities of her irrepressible children.

"Nuclear cloud? What are you bringing that up for?"

She opened her pocketbook and fished out a newspaper clipping.

"Nuclear disaster. That's what. If there's a leak, radioactive material will float over the hemisphere. I want you to give me a prescription. This article says that iodine drops can protect their thyroid glands against cancer."

"Molly," I reasoned with her, "there hasn't been any trouble since Chernobyl. You can't spend your life like Henny Penny. It's fine to be cautious, but there's a limit."

"You can't be too careful, Doctor. Here's something else I read. Those artificial sweeteners they put in everything these days. They're dangerous too. Like a time bomb. Someday something can happen."

Her youngest one was lying on the office floor as we talked. Molly continued her diatribe. The two oldest children were wrestling at the other end of the room.

"Give me a hand, will you?" I asked. "I can't get Brandon still long enough to get a peek at his ears. You said he's been complaining that they hurt him."

Molly came back to my level long enough to restrain Brandon.

"They're plenty red," I said. "I'd better put him on an antibiotic. He may have a rough night so I'll order some ear drops too."

"Fine, Doctor. He has had quite a few bad earaches already. I wonder if it's from the formaldehyde in the insulating material at our house?"

"That's one on me Molly. No more clippings, I'll take you word for it."

In spite of the decades that separated us, Molly and I got along very well. Her unorthodox views were dissimilar from mine, but we managed to find common ground where her children were concerned. I don't think I could have remained sane if all of the mothers were as unusual as Molly, but it was refreshing to have her in my practice.

CHAPTER 17

❧

Sharon and the Angel

It was a slippery night in January. I was relaxing at a Pediatric dinner, waiting to listen to a lecture on some current topic when my beeper went off. I had asked my answering service to reach me if Sharon, a child with cystic fibrosis, was any worse. The message was that she was breathing with difficulty, and I was needed right away.

After being greeted at the door, I pulled off my boots. tossed my coat and hat on a chair, and followed the family to the patient's room.

Sharon was propped up on two pillows, an oxygen mask flowing some relief to her damaged lungs. I reached for my stethoscope, observed her chest move up and down, but could hear little air enter or leave. Much of her life had been spent in this room lately. The ravages of her illness were evident and I saw that her barrel chest couldn't keep up with her body's demands. I noticed her stained teeth, her protuberant abdomen, her wasted buttocks and clubbed fingers. Her lips were dusky and those spindly arms and legs were cold and blue. Sharon's eyes scanned my face briefly, and then she closed them and seemed to drift into unconsciousness.

Sharon had been doomed from birth. Her oldest brother had died during infancy and two other children had succumbed also to this genetic nightmare. Three who had been spared the slow execution from cystic fibrosis were part of the witnessing circle that watched this painful sickroom scene.

I motioned to her father to follow me and we went downstairs to the kitchen.

"You were right to call when you did. You've done all you can here. Sharon will have to go to the hospital."

He nodded and was ready to return to his daughter's side when I realized that his wife was nowhere to be seen. He picked up my obvious surprise that Sharon was nearing the end of her impossible struggle without her mother at her side. The years of caring for her had been made easier with that quiet woman at hand, always there to buffer the pain and futility of our efforts with her reassuring confidence.

I followed Sharon and her father to the hospital. She was hustled into her room by the nurses who had known her so well during other crises. Then we had a chance to talk. He looked spent and in need of sleep.

"Sandy just couldn't stand it any longer. That's all there is to tell you, Doctor. This morning when Sharon got so bad, we decided to call you. After that my wife ran down the stairs and left the house. She hasn't called since. Just took off in our old station wagon."

There wasn't much that I could say. We went back to the dying child, but our vigil wasn't very long. Sharon stopped breathing that night.

I was leaving the hospital when I saw Sandy in the waiting room. She sat, Bible in hand, gazing vacantly ahead. She called to me as I passed by.

Her appearance was surprising. No sign of emotion, no tears, no clue to the torment that must have overpowered her. Then she spoke, very calmly I thought.

"It's over? She didn't suffer too much at the end, did she?"

"It was peaceful. Really it was."

"Thank God. Did she ask for me, Doctor?"

"Not while I was there."

"Come sit down a minute," Sandy said. "I'd like to talk about something that's important to me . . . about Sharon."

We settled in the chairs. I wondered why she didn't run to her husband's side to share the grief. Poor man. He needed more than the priest and I could offer.

"You think I'm an unnatural mother, don't you?" she began. "I've made this trip three times before, you know. I wouldn't go out for a cup of coffee then. I sat by my children and watched and watched. My grip was all that seemed to keep them here. And then they were gone."

She shifted restlessly. "With Sharon I could see we were heading the same hopeless way as with the others. I know you did all you could, Doctor. Those new antibiotics pulled her through a couple of times and Mike and I kept reading about longer lives for kids with cystic fibrosis. Hope for the future." She touched her chest. "In here, I knew it was whistling in the dark. It would never happen in Sharon's lifetime."

"I must say you covered up beautifully. You used to amaze me. You were so up-beat all the time."

Sandy managed a little smile. "I had to for Mike and the kids, as well as Sharon," she said, "but I knew how it would end . . . I didn't know when the end would be."

She stopped and again a smile lit up her face.

"A couple of weeks ago, a wonderful thing happened. Sharon came into our bed. She was so excited. She told us that she had been sleeping. You know how noisy that compressor is. The one for the mist tent. Well, it was quiet in her room. Not a sound. At the foot of her bed, she saw a tall, beautiful angel."

"An angel," I echoed.

"He looked like one of the angels on the church windows. Kind and loving. He held out his arms to her. Then he took her by the hand. 'Where are we going?' Sharon said she asked. 'Mommy, he told me it was time for me to go with him to another place . . . a perfectly wonderful place.' "

"That's some story and some dream. Was there more?"

"Sharon was changed so, Doctor," Sandy said. "You can't imagine the difference in that child. She crawled in bed between us that night. There wasn't any fear left. It wasn't like the others when they were failing."

Sandy closed her eyes and seemed to forget that I was there.

"She had trust that a gentle friend would come for her sometime. So did I. Tonight I didn't have to be with my baby."

I listened to the fairy tale intently. Sandy was at peace this time. It took a dream to change the way she looked at the final days of her child's life. I had been troubled by her apparent abandonment when she ran away from Sharon, but I was wrong in my judgment. I had to learn more about the way people grieve. Sandy needed no defense for her commitment to her family. An act of faith had allowed her to accept her loss with less outward emotion. That was more healing than I could provide.

CHAPTER 18

∾

Sarah and the Rabbits

Every profession builds a wall around itself. The terms that define its parameters are puzzling and seem to be a private language. The growth of new technologies has increased these strange tongues and has made most of us feel like outcasts in fields other than our own.

I was baffled by computers but their use in medicine compelled me to make an effort to understand how to operate them. During a visit to our grandchildren during the mid-1980's, I watched my seven-year-old grandson solve the mysteries with ease. He flicked a switch, inserted a floppy disc, and sat in front of the monitor. He touched the keyboard gently and selected an item from the menu. His fingers darted swiftly and before long the screen was covered with charts and figures. There was a harmony between the child and the machine. How I envied the confident way my grandson interacted with the computer. He scarcely noticed I was there until he had entered his final sentences. Then he pressed a key and commanded the printer to copy the entire page.

He turned to me as the message appeared. "Grandpa, it's easy. Would you like me to show you?"

The simple science of the computer with its jargon of funny words was too complex for me to grasp in a single session. I nodded as he rattled off the technique of word processing and wondered if I would ever be computer literate.

My difficulties with this tool of modern communication made me sympathize with my patients. Doctors are as guilty as any professionals in using a secret kind of speech, understood by one another but a puzzle to everyone else.

The Grants were among those who were benefited by the better understanding of some childhood diseases. Their baby came screaming into the world, a sparkling, late addition to their life. Mrs. Grant, a frail, middle-aged woman, had the baby cradled and was exchanging the pleasantries mothers coo to their newborns, when I stopped in her room.

"I thought you'd like to know about your daughter," I said. "She's a big girl, nearly eight pounds and she's twenty inches long. The nurses say she takes her feedings right down and she's only down a few ounces from birth weight. All in all, a good report."

"Thank you, Doctor. I just love to hold her. She's so sweet and cuddly."

"I checked her for the first time yesterday but you were sound asleep when I came in. Didn't want to disturb you. Today there was a little change in her skin color. Did you notice it?"

"Yes, a kinda tea rose. Is that something to worry about? Is there anything wrong, Doctor?"

"Well, it can be a problem. She's getting jaundiced. Do you know what jaundice is?"

Mrs. Grant shook her head.

"It's common during the first days of life. Quite a few things cause it Some are not serious, but others need a special kind of treatment."

"Doctor, I don't understand. What's the yellow from and what do you have to do?"

"It all depends. You've been pregnant before. Was the last one yellow?"

"No. My first baby was fine when she was born. But we all had some kind of bug when she was two months old. She picked it up and they said it was pneumonia she died of."

"It must have been awful on you. It takes a long time to get over something like that. How about the next time? This baby's your third pregnancy, isn't she?"

"Yes. The third one. But I had a miscarriage. It was during the war and we were always moving around. I didn't feel good right from the start and lost one at about the third month."

"Then what happened?"

"Oh, we moved up here and split up. That's when I met Joe. We lived together for a time and what do you know . . . after so many years I was pregnant again."

"Any troubles this pregnancy?"

"None at all. I'm older than most of the women having babies. So I was very careful with what I ate and I walked a great deal. The doctor said I was a good patient."

"That's great. Now, how about your husband? What about his

health?"

"He's a tough old nut. He works awfully hard, driving a cab and trying to make ends meet. You have to put in long hours and Joe's not young any more. He's pushin' sixty."

She smiled. "It's such a thrill for him to be a father. Never had a kid before. He's a whole lot different from my first man. Joe cares what happens to me," she said proudly, "and he's crazy about the baby. To think we're gonna have this joy so late in our lives. Doctor, you should've seen that guy after the baby was born. He had to scrub his hands and wear one of those gowns before he could hold her. What a sight! He was afraid to move. Thought she might break."

"I know how he feels. I was like that with our first. But here's the problem with Sarah—that's what you named her, isn't it? Sarah's getting yellow. That's what jaundice is, yellowing of the skin. That's because there's difference in blood groups between you and the baby."

She looked at me blankly.

"See, there's something in her blood that's present in your husband and not in you. The baby gets a gene from each parent. This gene is called the Rh factor."

I continued with my explanation. "Mrs. Grant, you're Rh negative. During pregnancy your body makes antibodies against this Rh positive factor the baby got from Joe. They wrap around the baby's blood cells and start to break them down. The baby turns yellow and yellower. That comes from the pigment, the coloring matter that leaks out when the red blood cells are damaged."

Poor Mrs. Grant didn't have a chance. I knew I couldn't explain it in terms she could grasp. Finally I said, "But there is a treatment. We can stop the further breakdown of blood by removing part of the baby's blood and replacing it with some from a donor; from our blood bank."

"I still don't understand what you're talking about. Maybe Joe and I can sit down with you a little later. He's better'n me at medical stuff."

"Of course. I intended to tell both of you about Sarah anyway. Can you reach him now?"

"I think I can. I'll have him called at work and he can come right up."

"Good. You'd better do that because I want to talk to both of you about an exchange transfusion. That's what can help the baby."

"An exchange transfusion?" The bewildered woman appealed to me, "Please talk to Joe and me together, will you?"

"Certainly. In the meantime, better get the baby back to the nursery."

She picked Sarah up and planted a kiss on her forehead. We waited for Joe to reach the hospital but our discussion didn't help very much. They were lovely, uneducated people. The concept was too big for them.

"The treatment," I told them, "consists of an operation. We have to place a plastic tube into the navel; right where the blood vessels go to and from the afterbirth. We thread this tube into the baby, take out a little of the baby's blood cells which are Rh positive, and replace them with an equal amount of Rh negative bank blood. We do this over and over, watching Sarah all the while. It takes an hour or so."

They signed a permit although they really didn't understand. They had faith I knew what I was doing. I'm sure they were comforted that I had done the operation many times before.

Little Sarah did well and at one week of age was ready to go home. All the nurses crowded around as Joe took his special cargo home and I promised to stop by in a few days and take a look at Sarah.

The Grants lived in a walk-up flat near the center of the city. I climbed the stairs, knocked on the door, and was invited in. To describe it as a home would be to dignify their living space with too generous a term. A hovel in total disarray would be more appropriate.

There was no furniture other than a card table, two wooden chairs, a coffee table and a radio on the mantel of the unusable fireplace. A space heater was the main source of heat for the entire place. No hot water and a kitchen with an ice box and a two burner stove. The bedroom space was as leanly furnished as the rest of their quarters.

Sarah slept in a large orange crate with several blankets under her and a small pillow supporting her head.

"I'm glad you could come, Doctor," she said to me. "I've been waiting for you to explain, now that it's over, what caused Sarah's troubles. I don't understand it, you know."

"Well, let me look her over first," I said.

We took the baby out to the front room, placed the card table by the window, stripped her down. Everything was back to normal. Her color was good. She was active, cried lustily and then sucked like mad on the pacifier her mother stuck in her mouth.

Mrs. Grant watched intently as I felt for the liver and spleen, looked at the eyes, listened to the heart and went through the whole ritual of a pediatrician's exam.

"Too bad Joe's not here," I said. "I'd like to tell him how Sarah's doing and go over the mysteries you've been wondering about."

I heard a scratching sound and over in the corner noticed something I'd missed when I first came in.

There was a large cage at one end of the room. The door was open and I saw a rabbit hopping towards us and saw traces of the pellets he excreted, tucked against the corner of the cage, some trailing after him.

What could I tell this mother? How could I explain the technology that had allowed us to help her child overcome the first hurdle of her life? Where could I begin? I took a deep breath and went through my pat sermon again, knowing that she would smile and thank me and wouldn't understand, anymore than I could understand how anyone could live in such squalor.

Sarah survived. Joe didn't. He died when she was ten years old, and I saw little of Sarah until her first baby was delivered.

A proud grandmother looked through the nursery window at her grandchild and smiled at me when I announced that everything was fine.

"Not yellow, huh, Doctor?" she asked.

"No, not a bit yellow. He's a great looking boy."

He was, as were the next three children. Nice looking, healthy, dirty, smelly, unkempt children. Sarah's man, Jimmy, was devoted to his expanding family and, although he couldn't provide very well financially, he was caring and attentive. He was there when one of the children was ill or needed immunizations, while Sarah seemed overwhelmed and stayed at a distance.

One day, Jimmy called and asked to bring his youngest child to the office. The baby had been feverish, was feeding poorly, and he cried constantly.

The nurses, knowing the family, placed them in a room with good ventilation. I took a look at the plump eight-month-old.

It was true. He was very ill. His face was bright red, eyes cracked at the creases. His lips were parched and bleeding, just as Jimmy said. A rash covered his chest and abdomen. His fingers were swollen and the tips were purplish. Temperature 104° and he was inconsolable. His throat was inflamed and the glands on either side of his neck were enlarged visibly—he winced as I touched them.

His skin was a mess. The diaper area was beefy red with areas of ulceration where the urine had scorched the skin. It was clear he hadn't been bathed very often and his diaper was gringy and discolored.

I stared at the sick child, reviewing the many possible causes for his troubles.

There is a disease that had been identified during the last decade which resembled the baby's clustering of symptoms. It is called Kawasaki's disease and carries a high risk for long term complications, even survival. In this strange disease even young children may develop coronary artery damage.

It was necessary, of course, to hospitalize young Steven and treat this bizarre condition.

It was *deja vu* time. I looked at Sarah and Jimmy and at Mrs. Grant in the hospital waiting room. When I tried to explain to the anxious family what caused Steven's problems, I couldn't help being transported back a few years. I thought of the day I visited Sarah at home and watched rabbits bouncing across the floor.

Rh problems or Kawasaki's disease. Medical breakthrough and exciting discoveries. Young children being challenged by strange sicknesses but the special language to make it all clear, waiting to be invented.

CHAPTER 19

❧

Tianga

It is hard for me to believe that dealing with people could ever be ordinary or monotonous. There was never a day in all my years of Pediatrics that did not have unexpected turns. Conflicts between siblings, parents and teachers; catastrophic illness, suicide were dumped in my lap. Many times there was an undercurrent that was easy to detect; at other times, a surprise leaped out during a routine visit.

Tianga had been bothered by constipation and had discussed means of treatment with one of my partners at a recent office call. The usual methods weren't working and she was back again with her mother, waiting to talk about this annoying problem.

They were in my consultation room. Tianga, already in one of the ridiculous paper gowns that we provide for maturing girls, was relaxing on the examining table. She was quite composed, but her mother seemed extremely upset. Mrs. Jackson was an immense woman whose bulk filled the large armchair near my desk. She wouldn't make eye contact with me or her daughter, but remained head bowed, focusing on some design on her shoe or the carpet.

Tianga began. "Same business, Doctor. It's no better. The mineral oil and that other awful tasting stuff . . . nothing worked."

"I see. Maybe it's not as bad as you think. Lots of young people your age have the same complaint. Did you know that? Anyway, I think there's too much fuss over regular movements."

"She's having bad cramps, though, Doctor. That can't be right."

"Are they worse near your periods? I think you started earlier than a lot of girls. You were ten, weren't you, when you had your first period?"

"Just after my birthday. Sometimes there's more discomfort in the middle of the cycle. Not due to constipation and it's not serious either."

I looked at her health record and commented, "You're twelve and a half. The last time you were weighed you were one hundred and five pounds and you were five feet and one inch. Just right. You don't skip meals, do you?"

"No, she doesn't. I make sure she has a good breakfast before she goes to school and she buys lunch every day. She gets lots of greens and fresh fruits. Like the other doctor said."

Mrs. Jackson still studied her shoes. "Tianga's not here for her bowels, Doctor."

"Oh, I figured she was. That's what she said at the start."

"It's her period. She hasn't had it since Thanksgiving."

"Since Thanksgiving? That's nearly three months. She's always been regular?"

"From the beginning. Every twenty-eight days. Goes on the calendar." Mrs. Jackson opened her purse and found her notebook. "I mark it in the front of this book. Last time was November 27th and the one before was October 30th and so on."

"All right. It happens if you exercise a good deal. You know, gymnastics, distance running, nutty diets . . . can change your patterns. Sometimes sickness . . . mono, anemia and so on. Or, of course, pregnancy."

I swallowed and glanced at the impassive mother and then at her young daughter.

"Have you had contact, sexual contact, since November?"

Tianga's had bobbed up and down. "Once, just once. It was a couple of days before Christmas. During the vacation."

Mrs. Jackson let out a sigh. "What do you think, Doctor? I mean about the constipation and the periods and all that?"

I wasn't about to trivialize any of this. I buzzed for my nurse.

"Let's get a urine sample from Tianga. Then she can sit in the waiting room while I talk to Mrs. Jackson."

Tianga jumped down, kissed her mother and followed the nurse. Then Mrs. Jackson turned her chair facing me and raised her head. There was despair, defeat and pain in her eyes . . . something you could sense even without the likelihood of her daughter's pregnancy.

"The urine sample. That's to test for pregnancy. You know that. But if it's positive . . . and it probably will be, then we'll have to make some plans."

She buttoned her sweater all the way to the top even though beads of sweat glistened on her forehead. Again a giant shudder of a sigh escaped.

"Supposing it was your daughter, Doctor? What would you want to do?"

"It's hard to say. Everybody's situation is different, I guess."

"Yes. Probably. But I'm alone and I can't think straight. This whole mess can't be happening. Not to her." She paused and then said, "Do you think because I'm black and a single parent that this is something that should be expected?"

I started to protest. She cut me off.

"That's what somebody might say . . . I really don't mean you. Oh, I don't know why I'm talking like this!"

Mrs. Jackson accepted the Kleenex and wiped her eyes. She was dressed neatly in a gray outfit. The cardigan sweater covered a lovely cameo locket. Her hair had islands of silver and was coifed carefully. She had an attractive, full face without a wrinkle or a line and despite her size, moved gracefully and carried herself with dignity.

"I didn't have Tianga until I was thirty-seven years old, and I was married. My mother was thirty-seven when I was born. So, you can see she wasn't brought up to be wild. I watched her everywhere she went. Took her to church. I knew where she was all the time. Did I tell you she was an honor student?"

"I believe you did, one other time. You can be proud of her. These are crazy times though. Things happen . . . they happen to so many. You've tried your best."

She didn't seem to be listening to anything I said. Just a body in the room with a huge load to carry.

"She'll be sitting out there reading a comic book. I don't know what to do. Course I know when it happened. The boys and girls were around the table in my dining room. They used to come over to our place after services. I was in the kitchen. Gettin' things ready . . . you know . . . cookies and some cola. The kids were talking and laughing. Nice bunch. Then some fellows I hadn't seen before came in. Stayed there for awhile. They ate the cookies, listened to some of that rock music and everybody got up to leave. All but one mean-looking guy. Tianga and I cleared the table and I started to wash the dishes."

There was a different tone to her voice. A belligerence that was noticeable. She went on.

"Tianga had gone to her room. The door was closed and when I went in, she was standing in front of the mirror, fooling with her hair and he was lying on her bed . . . with his leather boots on, watching everything she was doing . . . and sweet-talking her all the time. I got mad and told him to get out of her room that minute. I didn't want anybody in there. I wanted him to leave and I wanted her door wide open."

"Good for you. So he left?"

"He did not. He just stared at me and laughed. He said he'd leave when he was good and ready and when Tianga wanted him to. Then he got up, took hold of me and steered me out of the room. He had a knife . . . with a switchblade kind of thing. He pulled it out of his pocket and said that was the only chaperone he needed . . . didn't need me around. He locked the door."

"Did Tianga yell or anything? Did she try to stop him when he was forcing you out of the room?"

"She was afraid of him . . . that he might get nasty. With the knife and all."

"Couldn't you get help?"

"Doctor, I banged on that door with all my might and said I'd call the police. But he knew I wouldn't. Not as long as he had that knife. He would have used it on my baby."

I went over to the unhappy woman. It didn't seem like the time to say much more. "We might as well find out if Tianga's urine test for pregnancy was positive before talking about options."

We figured she was about eleven weeks pregnant when the laboratory confirmation came back the next day. Tianga was still in school when I spoke to her mother.

"There are a few choices, Mrs. Jackson. She can go through with the pregnancy. She can have an abortion or she can have the baby and then it can be put up for adoption. But wait a minute. You told me you were a single parent. Where is her father? Do you know?"

"He hasn't seen her in two years, maybe more. He sent her a birthday card last year, but he doesn't give a damn about either of us. Never gave me a penny. He just walked away. He said he couldn't be tied down."

"It's up to you . . . if you don't think he should help you with this."

"Doctor, he's as mean as the one who got her pregnant. He'd blame me for what happened. It wouldn't do any good. No, as always, it'll be Ti and me."

"O.K. But you and Tianga will have to decide real soon. And no matter, she'd best see an OB man. Teenage pregnancies need extra special care."

"Soon as she comes home from school. Doctor, she's a child herself. Too young to have a baby."

Mrs. Jackson wrestled with the decision. Tianga begged her mother to let her have the child. Together they would be a perfect team. Please,

please, please, Momma. I couldn't intrude in their lives other than to cite a few statistics about what could happen to infants whose mothers were so young.

My phone rang. "Doctor, another question. Do we have to let that guy know she's pregnant? He's the father. He may not let her have an abortion. What do you think?"

"Listen to me," I said. "He hasn't any rights. He stuck a knife in your face and raped you daughter. That's the way the law would figure it. If I know his kind, he'll be far gone by now. You'll have no trouble with him."

"That's a relief. Make the appointment with the OB man, please. Tianga cried a lot. She doesn't want to kill the baby. But it isn't the right way for her to be a mother. Please God, some day, when she's older . . . not now."

CHAPTER 20

࿔

Lucille's Trap

There are some events that are so painful that they are kept buried deep in the mind's corners. They remain submerged like tuberous bulbs, but the flowers they produce are often ugly. What happened to this patient of mine, I'll call Lucille, was so unbelievable that I've hesitated to bring it to light.

Lucille was the only girl in a family of five children. She came along after three brothers and was given as much attention as her mother could spare. The boys were typical roughnecks and Lucille dodged most of the physical violence and concentrated on frilly clothes, dolls and her books. She spent hours in her room with "Anne of Green Gables" and "Little Women" propped up in front of her and with a dishful of brownies for snacking. Her father set aside a half an hour each night for quality time with her. Together they let their imaginations roam and enjoyed fantastic stories of heroes and heroines, of great adventures and dreams to be fulfilled. It was the sunniest part of her day.

Even this small treasure that she shared with her father was lost when another brother was born. I discovered the new baby had a loud heart murmur and realized he would need a series of operations to survive. I arranged for him to be transferred to a medical center several hundred miles away where favorable results were being reported with this type of malformation.

While her parents were away, her brothers stayed with one set of grandparents and Lucille with the other. She was bused to school every day and had no chance to be with the friends near her home. It was a lonely period for her, but she was the center of a doting grandmother's life and a companion for her grandfather. He had been forced to retire when the uncertainties and pressure of the stock market were thought to be too much for his hypertension and recurrent heart failure. He missed the lightning decisions he used to make at the brokerage house.

Instead he was isolated, like his granddaughter, away from friends and pulse-tingling activities, sentenced to nothing more thrilling than reading the seed catalogue (and that after his morning dose of Valium). Perhaps Lucille's presence could brighten his days.

Lucille's baby brother spent two months in the hospital before he could return home. He still needed hours of care and it was decided to have both sets of grandparents continue their temporary guardianship since there had been enough disruption of routines. They would finish the term and then the family could be reunited.

The baby was growing well and was ready for the repair of his cardiac defect during the summer. Lucille begged to go with her parents this time. She reasoned that school was out and since her father could be away from work on weekends only, she could keep her mother company. She was hugged and thanked for the offer but was told to stay with her grandparents. They'd pray that the baby would be able to be a regular part of their family before long.

"You'll be seeing Lucille B. this afternoon, Doctor," my secretary announced. "She's extra. We have the time. Your two o'clock cancelled, so you'll be able to examine her little brother and her."

"Did we get all the reports form Philadelphia?" I asked.

"They came in yesterday. He's to see you for a regular check-up. Then he goes to the Center for the cardiologist. They'll keep in touch with the surgeon about drug dosages and all that."

"We've done that before. I guess it's the age of the specialist . . . I suppose it's best for the patient. But what's Lucille's trouble? Did her mother say?"

"No . . . just that she's been losing weight?"

Lucille clung to her mother from the moment she walked into the office. My staff picked up the change in her right away. No smiling eleven-year-old this time, but a sullen girl who protested being weighed and measured and was on the verge of tears all the while. She watched me examine her little brother but refused to let the nurse prepare her when her turn came.

"Mother, there's nothing wrong with me. I don't want to be here. Let's go home."

"Honey, we're just making sure you're O.K. You've lost a lot of weight—ten pounds while we were away with the baby."

"I don't care. I'll be fine now that you're back."

Dorie B. turned to me and said, "Doctor, she always liked my mother's cooking better than mine. It used to make me jealous. Grandma made the best Spanish rice and coconut cream pie.

There was something about Lucille that frightened me. I had seen enough adolescents to know that they often went through periods of depression. Their black moods were hard to alter. A wall seemed to grow, separating them from anyone but their peers.

I asked a few questions, probing as delicately as I could. What was behind the mask of resentment would have to be extracted slowly.

"Have you been doing anything special this summer? Swimming, camping?" I fumbled.

"A little. Grandma's got a pool."

"Are you glad to be back with your brothers? Now that your folks are home?"

"You must be kidding. Those creeps are a pain. I didn't miss them."

" Well, how about those books? Did you read much? I heard that you are a great reader."

Lucille started to cry. She threw her arms around her mother and pleaded with her.

"Please, Mamma. I want to go home. Let's go. Then you can have Billy examined at the hospital. I don't feel good."

They left; Lucille was still sobbing. Her mother carried the baby and half-dragged her unhappy daughter with her.

I returned Dorie's phone call that evening. She apologized for Lucille's strange behavior and repeated her concern about the nasty streak she had noticed in the child.

"She's been impossible these last few weeks, Doctor. Her brothers aren't angels, heaven knows, but the slightest remark from them and she flies off the handle. And her Daddy . . . she's been so close to him . . . if he as much as asks her about school or how she feels . . . she dissolves in tears and runs to her room."

"I think it's important that she get some help," I said. "That child is bothered, depressed, whatever label you give it. She's going through a crisis."

"But why?" Dorie asked. "I know we were gone longer than we thought we'd be. But she's always loved being with my father and mother. They give her the V.I.P. treatment. As a matter of fact, they were so worried about Lucy that when my father went for his weekly follow-up, he asked about her eating and her personality change."

"I see. Anything found wrong?"

"Dad's doctor gave her some extra vitamins and said we should talk to you if she wasn't picking up."

"It's not that simple," I said. "Believe me, she needs more than vitamins. I wish you'd get some counseling for her. Now is the time. Before it gets worse."

"I'll talk to my husband. But I can tell you Dennis doesn't think much of psychiatrists . . . if that's what you think she needs. He says they're full of hot air."

"Keep in touch," was all I could say.

They dragged their feet, as I knew they would. Nothing was done, and Lucille withdrew more and more from the family. The care of her little brother still occupied her parents' minds, and the children had to be dispersed once again to the grandparents for Billy's final trip to Philadelphia. Billy was to be discharged from their cardiac program if he passed his re-evaluation studies.

Lucille again balked at staying with her mother's parents. Her father collected her books and suitcase and deposited her bodily at their door. She ran to the house, snapped a goodbye to her father and sat on the steps, pouring out her laments to her grandmother.

"I love you Grammy," she exclaimed. "Can we be together . . . you and me?"

They carried her overnight case and library books to her room. Her grandmother spent the morning outlining plans for the activities.

"Lucy, we're going to have fun together . . . starting tomorrow. Look at the places I've lined up for you. I've a bridge club this afternoon. Grandpa will be here. You won't be lonesome."

"Grandma, I need you. Do you have to go?"

"They're expecting me. They couldn't find a fourth. So I can't let them down. But I told them to get someone else for next week."

"I think I'll stay in my room until you get home. O.K.? I'm very tired."

"Suit yourself. I'll be back before you know it."

I never got the whole story. Lucille couldn't be aroused when her grandmother came home. A bottle of Valium was at her bedside. She spent the night in the hospital but gradually grew more alert and was allowed to leave. She refused to discuss her reasons for taking the pills. Her grandfather said he had knocked at her door and offered her some hot chocolate in mid-afternoon. When she didn't answer, he entered the room and found her.

Lucille's mother and father asked to meet with me. It was more than a week after the nearly-successful suicide attempt.

"We should have listened to you," Dennis began. "It's the lousiest business . . . couldn't imagine anything worse."

Dorie took over. "Lucy came to the nursery. I had been feeding the baby. It was right after we got home. Poor kid. She looked just awful. She stood near the crib . . . wanted to tell me something. I could see that. Then it all came out."

"Doctor," her husband said, "her Dad has been sick a long time. You knew that. He's got high blood pressure and he's had a bypass. He takes a lot of medicine. The Valium was his and there's a lot of other stuff in the medicine cabinet."

Dennis went on. "He's acted real funny since he had to quit work . . . not the way he used to be. Damn it, Doctor, he was doing things to Lucy. Touching her, weird stuff. He must have been out of his head . . . from the medicine probably. Lucy said he'd been doing it every time he could get her alone."

Dorie interrupted him. "Oh, Doctor, my father . . . he's such a fine man . . . it's hard to believe. But Lucy doesn't lie. She loves him. But she knew it was terrible . . . what he was doing. She felt dirty. That's why she wanted to die!"

I waited until they had control.

"Two things. Each very important. Lucille first. She will have to be seen by a psychiatrist immediately. I know a good one. Maybe things can be set straight . . . so she won't feel isolated again. That's when kids feel it's hopeless. As for her grandfather. He's a very troubled man, of course. And he has to be faced, by you and the Child Protective Agency. It's the law, Dorie. I have to report any sexual molestation."

"How awful! He'll be so ashamed. What about my mother? She doesn't know about any of this."

"It'll be better if you talk to her, Dorie. Rather than someone from the Children's Bureau."

Dennis put his arm around his wife.

"You're right, I guess. We'll get started. I'll go over and see my father-in-law. Dorie can break the news to her Mom. She's at our house now with Lucy."

The ending was strange, as was the whole episode. Dorie waited for an opening to tell her mother what had happened while Dennis drove over to confront his father-in-law.

He told us that night that he tired to hold back his anger as he sat in the study. He refused an offer of white wine and watched as the older man drank his slowly.

"Pop," he finally said, "you're gonna hear me out. We know what you've been doing. Lucy told Dorie. She told her why she was afraid to stay here and why she took the pills."

There was no denial. "Oh, Dennis, I'm glad it came out! I wouldn't have hurt Lucy for the world. It's a craziness. I don't know what happens. Something drives me."

He threw his glass against the wall and walked toward his son-in-law.

"Dennis, have someone help me. Give me strength."

His face grew livid. He put his hand to his forehead.

"There's a pounding inside. A heavy hammer keeps pounding."

His eyes rolled up and his body stiffened. Then he let out a cry and toppled to the floor. Dennis crouched over the fallen figure. The old man was breathing stertorously, his face twisted to one side.

The attendants lifted him onto the stretcher and carried him to the ambulance.

"It's a stroke, sir. His whole right side. They'll tell you more later on. Sometimes they make it . . . sometimes they're paralyzed and can't speak. As I said, the doctors will tell you more later."

Lucille's emotional distress took more time to resolve than her brother's heart defect. She appeared to have been aided by numerous sessions with the psychiatrist, but the long-term effect was uncertain.

CHAPTER 21

❧

Michael's Story

"Tell me, Doctor, isn't he cute? My husband loves his girls but we finally have a boy." Her black eyes admired the baby in her arms. "We'll call him Michael. We wanted to use that name twice before. Michael." She purred the name.

I stood quietly in front of the pair, mother and son, wondering how I could derail the rush of excitement.

"Has your husband been here today?" I might just as well face the two of them at once. She'd need someone to share the news.

"Not yet. He'll be here during visiting hours. You know last night he stood at the nursery window for over an hour. Just stared." She touched the newborn's cheek tenderly.

"See you tonight then." I retreated to the happier atmosphere of my office where I spent the afternoon inflicting fleeting pain with the indignities of booster shots and the like. I had little remorse for those necessary cruelties. It was the coming evening I dreaded.

Michael was kept in the nursery, in a far corner, cuddled by one of the nurses while I talked to his parents. Their room was filled with flowers and cards and presents (balls and bats and gloves, of course) were everywhere.

Michael's father pushed a box of cigars in my direction.

"What do you think of our boy, Doctor? Some kid, huh?"

"Sure, sure," I said. "Some kid."

Then I delivered my thunderbolt as gently as possible.

"It's hard to tell at first," I began. "You have to be experienced. Can't make a mistake. I've checked him over and over."

They both stopped me at once.

"What are you saying? What's wrong?"

They stared at me. I cleared my throat and said, "The baby really isn't all right. He looks perfect to you. But his muscles aren't strong and he'll never be like your other children. He'll be slow to walk and very slow in talking."

I paused. Their distress made me want to cry. But I had to go on.

"He'll always be simple, always a child in most ways."

"How can you tell us that?" screamed Michael's father. "What kind of devil are you? You're wrong. You're wrong!"

"No. I wish I could say he'll be fine. But he has mongolism. We call it Down's syndrome. And there's no doubt about the diagnosis."

I dialed the nursery number and told them to bring Michael to his mother's room. I went through the indisputable features of their infant's handicaps. They resisted the painful evidence with sobbing and cursing. Michael's father stared at the bassinet in front of him.

"Take him back," he begged the nurse. "We have to be alone." He waved everyone away and sat, deflated, beside his wife's bed.

By morning their minds were made up. Their baby would have to be considered dead. They could not bear the daily wounds of caring for their retarded son.

It wasn't that easy. Michael was born at a time when children who were developmentally delayed were no longer spirited to institutions. Instead they were blended into the family fabric. All the studies showed that the quality of life was enhanced if a child grew up with caring relatives. The power of this theory gained such momentum that no alternative program was available. No public facility would accept a child with Down's syndrome, and foster care or a sanitorium would cost more than the family could manage. So a weeping mother bowed to circumstances, and Michael became a member of their household.

Michael endeared himself to everyone. The prophecy was correct. He was affectionate and easy to raise in the early years. Even when another baby, a sister, entered the family, he still received constant attention. His grin won me over, and visits to my office were a shared treat. The teacher in the special education class reinforced the virtues of home care with her comments about his accomplishments.

"Hey, Doc, he's learned to catch a softball," said his Dad, while Michael stuck his fielder's mitt in my face. "Maybe he'll be an athlete after all."

They had stopped in my office for a consent form. The Special Olympics required a signed slip from the doctor certifying the athlete's state of health.

"After work I take him to the park," said the enthusiastic man. "We play catch. It didn't seem he'd ever get the hang of it. I must have thrown the ball a thousand times before he could get it right. But he didn't give up. He'd stick his glove up the way I showed him and, at last, our practice paid off. My boy's a real pro now."

They left the office and headed back to the park. They were going to work on his batting stance, his father said. Maybe if he became a better hitter, Michael would take his bat to bed with him at night. He already slept with his glove under the pillow.

But an unpredictable factor upset the serenity of their lives. Michael's father developed an increasing disability from emphysema, which made him unable to work. Their income from his small pension had to be supplemented by his wife's part-time job. With his mother away at work, Michael could not be supervised so closely and became belligerent. The docile child grew rebellious and difficult to control.

"Doctor, I'd like you to stop over and see Michael." I added his name to my list of after-hour visits.

"Such a bad thing," she said. "The neighbors brought him home today. He was bumped by a car a few blocks from here. He wandered away while I was at work. It doesn't look as though he's hurt badly, but please come."

Michael, not at all contrite, ran to the door when I rang. His smile was as broad as ever. He followed me to the bedroom, pulled open my bag and selected some instruments. Then he hopped on the bed, unzipped his shirt and waited for the familiar exam. There were no significant bumps or bruises, just a brush burn on his thigh.

We gathered in the kitchen and his parents poured out their grief. Michael sat near his father and basked in all the attention.

"He's changed. He won't listen anymore," said his mother. "It's not the first time he took off alone. My husband tried to stop him, but Michael, can you imagine, Michael kicked him and went out the door."

A chastened father, wheezing audibly, added to the history.

"The older girls are married. You know that because you take care of their kids. There's just Dawn at home with us. She helps a lot when my wife's at work." He stopped for breath. "But when Dawn's at school, it's the two of us." He gestured toward his son. "Would you believe he's stronger than I am?"

We sat mutely for a time. Then Michael's mother jumped up. "Where are my manners tonight? The coffee's perking and I forgot all about it."

She filled our cups and placed a dish of baklava on the table. Michael grabbed two pieces, stuffed them in his mouth and sat down again.

"You never gave me a clue," I said. "I didn't realize how bad it was. I'll call tomorrow and see if some relief can be found . . . a respite or a group home."

"My God!" was all the exhausted man could say. Then he added, "Twenty-one years with him."

Michael followed me to the door, then raced back for more sweets.

The social workers found a group home that was geared to handle young adults like Michael. They would try to teach him greater self-sufficiency. The program had worked well with others. Best of all, he would spend weekends at home with the family. Parting after twenty-one years would be unbearable. Under the circumstances it was the only way.

His mother and father wept when the bus arrived. Michael carried his suitcase on board and did not look back.

CHAPTER 22

❦

Foam

One of the great delights is the second generation family. It is a seal of approval when they run their finger down a list of pediatric specialists and decide they'll continue to cast their lot with me.

Terry decided to research the kind of care his child might get and paid visits to a number of other physicians in town. He and his wife had a clipboard with answers to key questions carefully tabulated. Do you object to pacifiers? What about circumcision? Do you believe in infant swimming programs? How about toilet training? When do you start immunizations and are they all necessary and safe as well?

I don't know what number I was in the interview department, but my answers must have matched their expectations. My score was high enough for them to engage me as their pediatrician.

There was a different twist to this prenatal conference. Terry and his wife were going to be adoptive, not biological parents. They had arranged for the social worker to bring the baby to my office right after birth. A physician for the adoptive agency would do the honors in the hospital and if the natural mother didn't change her mind at the last moment, the infant would be ready to enter their lives.

Terry and Anita arrived at my office an hour before the appointed time. They listened to the crying babies, heard siblings badger each other and watched the futile discipline exercised by short-tempered parents. Their testing would come soon enough, and they were anxious for it to begin.

In their wildest dreams, or nightmares, they would never have imagined the rough road they would have with Brian. He was one of the most active children I had ever seen. He shattered almost every record for motor development. By the time he was eight months old, he was walking. He had mastered climbing over the side rails of his crib by the first year.

Brian was fearless. Anita watched him plunge down the slide in the park and half expected to find him bruised and battered from his dare-devil adventures. She wanted to shield him from any possible hurt, but he moved with such speed that she found herself two steps behind and exhausted.

There were some mishaps. He had his share of stitches, even a broken leg, that delayed his attempts to ride his new two-wheeler. It was then, while his cast impeded his movements, that he discovered another form of entertainment. The pet cat permitted Brian to pummel her without scratching him. He grew bolder, apparently, and she finally gouged a small wound on his hand when he tried to flush her down the toilet.

He was different, I had to admit, and when Anita asked me if I thought Brian was hyperactive, I grinned and said maybe he was just exuberant. The premise that too much sugar or junk food was the basis for his constant movement didn't appeal to me. No miracles followed dietary restriction, I told Anita. She'd have to wait for him to change and hope for the best.

Brian had close ties with his father. He shadowed Terry, mimicking his every action, from digging in the garden to washing the car. The three-year-old was everywhere, ready to imitate anything he saw.

Anita devoted much of her office visit to stories about Brian's antics. She acknowledged there was humor beneath some of the more outrageous trials with her son.

"The other day," she told me, "I put Brian in his bed. Of course, he's in a junior bed . . . the crib's in the attic, ready for the next one, if we live through Brian's bringing up. I promised I'd be back when his naptime was over. He gave me a big hug, and of course, I melted. I always do. I closed the door and left."

"Terry had the day off and was painting trim on the second floor windows . . . on the other side of the house."

She stopped, took a deep breath, and then continued.

"He was nearly done when he felt a tug at his pant's leg. He looked down and there was Brian. He had gone right up the ladder. Nobody knew he wasn't in his room."

"Terry must have had a heart attack," I said.

"Darn near. He didn't know what to do at first. If he did the wrong thing, he thought Brian might fall . . . become frightened and lose his grip. So he acted as if he had expected him all along and told him to keep hold of his leg. He managed to lift Brian up to his level. Then he backed down the ladder, rung by rung."

Before long another child came along. A little girl for them to love and nurture. Brian trailed after Terry and Anita when they carried his new sister to the nursery. He was uncharacteristically subdued as his parents put the baby in her bassinet and tiptoed out of the room. He was ready for a playmate to share in his escapades, and when he realized that she was just a passive little infant, unable to do much other than yawn and gulp down formula, he lost interest.

Anita was thrilled to be able to nuzzle her daughter next to her and find that she didn't wriggle out of her grasp . . . that she could sit in the rocker and serenade the baby to sleep. There wasn't explosive volatility but a serenity foreign to Brian's temperament.

"Everybody's not the same," Terry kept reminding his wife. "It may have something to do with his genes. Probably Brian can't help acting the way he does. He's all boy. That's all. Be patient."

"Be patient? You've got to be a saint with that child. Our friends have boys, too. Nobody is like Brian. Terry, when I put him to bed at night . . . when he's bathed and shiny and sound asleep . . . I look at him and wonder how anyone could ever find fault with such a beautiful little child."

She listened for the baby. The nursery was quiet.

"I thought I heard her stirring. It's almost time to feed her again."

"Sweetheart," Terry said, "he's a marvelous little fellow. I'm sure he'll straighten out. Maybe we should send him to nursery school. It would give you a breathing spell."

"He's not ready. Three years old and still in diapers. He won't stay in one place long enough to be trained."

Anita brushed away her tears and went to the baby.

Terry walked past dump trucks and fire engines on his way to Brian's room. His son was nowhere in sight. There was a loud crashing sound from the bathroom and when Terry pushed the door open, Brian was lying motionless on the tile floor.

There was a swelling over his temple and foam was oozing from his mouth. His eyes were closed but he opened them and began to stir. The pinkish-white material kept pouring out.

Terry yelled for his wife and felt frantically for his son's pulse. It seemed full and regular. Brian tried to get up and then fell back.

When I arrived, they were still in the bathroom with Brian.

It wasn't difficult to piece together what had happened. Brian's curiosity had drawn him to the bathroom shelf. The assortment of bottles had an allure for him. He had loosened the cap on a giant-size bottle of shampoo and swallowed some. Then he lad lost his footing and had fallen to the floor, striking his head against the toilet.

By daybreak, he was as peppy as ever. There was no damage, but he kept blowing soap bubbles for the rest of the morning and to the amusement of his relieved parents, similar large bubbles came out the other end every time he passed gas.

Terry's forecast was accurate. Brian's impulsiveness diminished when he entered nursery school. The succeeding years were trauma-free and he transferred his energies to competitive sports. With his mellowing behavior, Anita felt less like a zookeeper and was able to delight in parenthood.

She and Terry had misgivings about the many programs aired on television dealing with adoptive children and their search for their true origins. In spite of all they had gone through to tame Brian and care for their daughter, they conceded the children's right to look for their biological parents.

Brian was playing a game of one-on-one when Anita called to him. His buddy waited with the basketball while Brian was invited to hear their proposition; a chance to find his roots.

He had been upset that the basketball game had been interrupted and wondered what discipline he was about to face. He was relieved to have an offer of help in looking for his "real" mother, not censure for some minor rule infraction.

Brian looked at his parents and then began to laugh. He raced across the room, hugged Anita and blurted out, "You thought I might like to find my mother. My gosh! Another mother. One mother is all that I can handle. Please don't wish another one on me!"

CHAPTER 23

∾

Better Living Through Chemistry

"There isn't anything wrong with my grandchild. A little chest cold. But it gave me an excuse to talk to you about Margaret. You've known her all her life, better than anyone else."

"She's all right, isn't she?" I asked. "I knew she was divorced but I figured she'd get along. She was a level-headed girl, as I remember her."

Mrs. Hogan turned to her grandson. "Charley," she suggested, "go read that book you were looking at, the one about dinosaurs. It's out in the waiting room. I want to talk to the doctor."

Charley was used to adult behavior. He hopped down quickly, waved at me, and said, "Gramma, remember I've got a ballgame this afternoon. Don't take forever."

She waved him away. "That fellow's no trouble. None at all. But neither was his mother at his age."

"I take it she's having a hard time. Well, so many couples are breaking up these days. She'll manage, though. She's smart and pretty. A hard combination to beat."

Her mother sniffled a few times and shook her head in denial. "You haven't seen her in a while, Doctor. You wouldn't recognize her. She's not the way she used to be. Not in the least."

She sat down, chest heaving and said, "Let me control myself, then I'll let you in on what's been happening to your favorite patient. Remember you used to tell her that she was your favorite patient?"

I flushed. "I guess so. But I'll have to plead guilty: I've said that to quite a few. She really was special, though."

"Sure. There was the usual baloney in the yearbook. Peppiest senior. Most likely to marry a millionaire. All that nonsense."

"Let me get her chart. It'll take but a minute and then we can talk."

She waited until the record of Margaret's first eighteen years was in my hands. The eldest of a family of seven. Good student, cheerleader, drama club, accepted at the State University. She had her last physical just before she went to college. On top of that, she was full of quick laughter and nice to look at.

Mrs. Hogan went on. "That's the way it was. Then she met Charley's father. He wasn't college material. I guess he worked at a stereo store and wasn't career oriented . . . that's the term they use, isn't it? Oh, they were serious about each other. He'd travel up to the college every weekend to see her."

"Sounds O.K. so far."

"It was in the beginning. But he had a few dollars to spend and she got carried away with all the parties. Something had to be neglected. She left college after one semester."

"No warning to you and her dad?"

"Yes. She said nothing she was studying was relevant to everyday life. Those were her words . . . not relevant."

"I'm surprised you couldn't persuade her. I know it's different now. But you seemed to have a good, solid relationship. As I recall, she was proud you were a nurse. I would have bet that she'd end up doing something in the health field. Nurse, doctor, lab technician."

"She wouldn't budge. Next thing we knew she moved in with this fellow . . . this Billy. We couldn't convince her to come home with us. It wouldn't have done any good anyway. She was all mixed up."

There was a pause before she managed a bit of a grin.

"At least she had the decency to get married."

"What did you think of Billy?"

"Never cared for him. Neither did her dad. But we figured she was doing the choosing."

I wasn't about to hurry her. Let the patients wait a little longer. Margaret wasn't under my care now, but her mother was so distressed that I had to let her ventilate.

"You knew she had Charley," Mrs. Hogan said. "You saw him in the hospital and I've brought him to you ever since. But you didn't know that Margaret and her husband didn't give that child any care at all. They were always dropping him off for me to watch. Sometimes I'd get a call from her asking me to keep him a couple of days. She wasn't feeling well. She'd say she had the bug or mono or some other deal."

"Did she have a job? Or was Billy earning enough to support them?"

"She had a job for about a month. She got a babysitter for Charley. But that didn't last very long . . . everything they earned they spent getting high. Pot, heroin, cocaine. You name it."

"Getting high. Pretty expensive habit."

"Yeah. Sure was. So expensive that her husband couldn't keep both of them going. He took off. Took off and she hasn't gotten a dime from him since."

She couldn't hold back any longer. I let her cry. There were plenty of tears that had been building up, and it must have been a relief for her to let them escape.

"Doctor, you can't imagine what's become of that girl. I'd go over there when I hadn't heard from her in days. She'd barely make it to the door. Charley'd be in his crib or playpen. Poor kid was half-starved. She'd actually forget to feed him. She was stoned most of the time."

"Couldn't you get her any help? Any counseling?"

"We tried. She promised to get into some kind of program. It never happened."

"How about Charley?"

"I'm coming to that. I got a call from her neighbor that Margaret had left him alone in the apartment. She'd been gone for hours and he was screaming. Poor boy. This time he was really starving."

"Did you report her for child neglect? You should have, you know."

"Maybe . . . but no, we didn't. We brought Charley to our house. We had the baby furniture and all. Then my husband went out to look for Margaret. He didn't know where to go first. We didn't know any of her friends. She had dropped out of sight. So, we called the police."

"Were they able to find her?"

"Oh, yes. She was in a shooting gallery. With a lot of other zombies. She'd gone there with some guy who had dough. We found out later she'd pick up with anyone who could afford what she wanted."

"But that was back quite a few years ago, wasn't it?"

"Yes. A few rotten years. She's been in and out of treatment centers. She's slept around; been in cheap rooming houses with the crummiest looking men you can imagine. She's had a baby that they've taken away from her. Some 'most likely to marry a rich guy' story."

"You've kept Charley. Did you adopt him?"

"We certainly did. The courts found his father He was as bad off as Margaret. So we had no trouble getting custody."

"Does Charley know any of this?"

"Some. He knows we're his grandparents. That his mother is sick and his father's left. That's it for now."

"Guess that's best."

Our discussion had ended when Charley knocked on the door.

"Grandma," he said, "I don't have all day. The ball game . . . remember? There's a ball game and I've got to change my clothes first."

Soon I had forgotten about Margaret, but one day a message arrived that involved me again. I was told there was an expectant mother in the maternity ward who wanted me to visit her. High risk pregnancies were hospitalized if there were complications such as toxemias or bleeding problems.

Margaret was in a large ward. She was sitting up in bed, reading a pulp magazine when she saw me.

"Over here," she yelled. "I'm the one who asked to see you."

As I neared her bed, she made a funny sound with her tongue. "You haven't changed a bit, Doctor. Ya look the way you did when I was growing up."

She looked at me a little longer and added, "Maybe your hair's grayer, but I could tell who you were the minute you came in."

"Good to see you. Same Margaret, aren't you?"

I felt guilty about lying. The eyes were the same, with hidden mockery and laughter. But her skin was thickened and yellow. Her dark hair needed brushing, and her hands shook as she tried to straighten the bedclothes. There were open sores on her forearms and a few scars on her fingers from forgotten cigarettes. Two upper teeth were missing; the gaps made me wonder what tooth fairy would place a reward under her pillow.

This was Margaret at thirty—the radiant person whose sparkle and charm had been so captivating. She had lost touch with the realities around her and tried to escape into a world of shadows and fantasy. The needle marks on her arms testified that she had blotted out the middle years of her youth. And now the last weeks of this pregnancy were being spent on methadone maintenance in the detoxification unit of the hospital.

We talked for a long time. Her frankness was remarkable. She told me about months when she went from pad to pad. She said she would swallow, snort or inject whatever was at hand. There were spaces in her memory that would never return. That was the part she minded the most, she told me.

"What the hell! That's history. This is another chance, Doctor. They said it was going better this time. I've been clean. Honestly. Only what's prescribed. Best of all, the baby's growing."

She pulled back the sheets and showed me the silhouette of her unborn baby.

"With your help, Doc, I can keep this one. Please be around when it's born. I'll be different if I can have this baby. Watch and see."

"I'll be there."

There wasn't much else I could say. I left her and went to pour over her voluminous clinic records. It took nearly an hour to wade through the maternity information.

Margaret was delivered by Caesarean section early the next month. The baby was hyperirritable for the first few days. She was a poor feeder and vomited most of what she swallowed. She had a high-pitched cry and made little jerky movements with her limbs. Once or twice she had spells when she wouldn't breathe for ten or fifteen seconds.

Sedatives ultimately controlled the baby's withdrawal symptoms and Margaret was allowed to hold her baby. She paraded all of her visitors to the nursery, extoling the beauty of her newborn. This time she knew she would be able to take her infant home.

She squeezed my hand when she was ready to leave. I told her she had done well, that I was proud of her. Margaret's voice had a strange, robotic sound. She measured her words like a careful apothecary.

"Isn't it wonderful? Can you believe she's all right, Doctor? Oh, I feel so good."

She stretched out the last word. Then she went on to say, "When I'm well, I'll take her out in the stroller. It may sound corny, but we'll see the sky and trees together and for the first time since I was a kid, I'll smell the flowers."

The baby occupied her life for the rest of the summer. I was hopeful she could do the impossible after a dozen years of addiction; especially when the social workers sent me favorable reports of her new lifestyle.

Mrs. Hogan called me some months later. She was very excited.

"Doctor, I need your help again. Margaret was telling me this morning that the baby has a fever. She doesn't know what to do. Of course I told her to sponge bathe the baby and give her some drops for the temperature."

"How's the baby now?"

"I don't know. I called Margaret a few minutes ago and she sounded very strange. Do you think you could make a call?"

"You think it's necessary? I'm in the middle of office hours."

"I'm really scared or I wouldn't ask you. I've got a funny feeling this time."

"All right. She hasn't moved again, has she? Is it the address that's on her chart?"

"It's the same place. But she doesn't always answer the bell. Says she's afraid of the neighborhood. If you don't mind, Doctor, I'll come by and we can go together. I have a key."

We didn't talk much on the way over. Mrs. Hogan twisted the strap on her pocketbook and hummed an unrecognizable tune.

"Turn at the corner. It's the second place on the right."

She unlocked the door of Margaret's flat and we went in. Nobody in sight. Absolute quiet, unbroken by a baby's cries.

Mrs. Hogan rushed ahead of me to the rear bedroom. Her daughter was sitting beside an empty crib, rocking back and forth, looking blankly at the wall.

"Where's the baby, Margaret? Where is she?"

Margaret didn't answer. Her mother ran from the room.

I heard a scream. "In here, Doctor! The baby's in here!"

Kimberly was in a half-filled bathtub, face down. I knew it was hopeless, but for ten minutes I tried to resuscitate the baby.

Mrs. Hogan sobbed. "I knew something was wrong. My God, this can't be. The little angel."

She wrapped the baby and carried her back to her crib.

"I'll have to notify the police and the coroner," I said. "Of course it was an accident, but they'll have a million questions. They always do."

When the police arrived Margaret still clung to her dead baby.

"Let them take Kimmie, honey. It's time for all of us to go."

"Oh, no. She's mine. They took the others away. This baby's mine."

Drug-related tragedies were not novelties any more. But my practice had been insulated until now. I grieved for the three generations who were destroyed by Margaret's addiction. I waited with Mrs. Hogan until the authorities finished their preliminary investigation. Margaret was not able to give a coherent account of the events leading to Kimberly's death, and stared at the questioning officer without saying a word. They sealed the apartment and took Margaret into custody . . . to be charged with infanticide.

CHAPTER 24

❦

Motherhood

She stood in the doorway momentarily and then followed her mother and her two babies into my office. Her mother deposited one of the children on the examining table, held the other snugly against her dirty tee shirt and sat down near my desk. My office nurse hovered protectively over the wheezing child and began recording his vital signs. The young woman drew a little closer but remained standing, not yet a part of the tableau.

These were new patients. My receptionist had received a call from the older woman earlier in the day and had asked that the children be seen promptly. They were, she said, having trouble breathing and wondered whether to take them to the emergency room immediately or have them examined in the office. I was seeing patients and she was told they could be evaluated without delay.

The older child was sitting upright when I approached him. He was a slender boy, about two and a half years old. He was wheezing audibly— his rib cage was moving up and down rapidly and he had a grunting sound with each breath out. His color was pale except for a tinge of blue around his lips and fingernails. His hair was matted and unkempt and his eyes were red-rimmed and swollen. A huge, weepy sore was on his upper lip and he kept touching it with his hand.

The nurse whispered to me, "Axillary temp is 100, respirations are 44/min., pulse 160," and stepped back. The boy looked up at me and did not appear to be frightened when I started to examine him. His grandmother carried the other child nearer to me and began to tell me about his present illness.

"He's been sick a lot, poor angel," she said. "He's with me most of the time, you know." She looked toward her daughter and continued. "Hazel has a hard time caring for these kids. They're only fifteen months apart. The little one was real early. They said he was just thirty weeks and with the trouble he had in the hospital and all that. He was in an incubator with tubes and IV's and then he had to have a monitor when he came home. She just couldn't handle all that and still go to school She's going to be a hairdresser when she's finished."

I held up my hand and motioned to the younger woman to come to the table. My nurse had brought a nebulizer and a face mask so we could start treatment. I finished a careful examination of his lungs, listened to his heart and held the breathing apparatus in place. We started the machine and waited for his respirations to improve.

"You'll need to learn how to use this set-up," I said. "He has asthma and he'll need round the clock care. Watch my nurse closely. She's an expert. It's not too hard once you've done it a few times."

Hazel glanced at her son and nodded. "Mom has asthma. She can take care of him at home. She knows how to use these things. I've got a couple more weeks until I get my license, so I can't do everything"

She stepped away and waited until the treatment was finished. Then it was the baby's turn. We weighed him, measured his length and head circumference, noticed his frail body with his pot belly and spindly legs. He had an inflamed eardrum, a slight cough and some congestion in his lungs also. Hazel was so different from her mother that she could have been a different species. She was tall and slender; every hair was in place, her makeup was professionally applied with long eyelashes, black lipstick, enameled fingernails, dangling earrings with high black boots part of the picture. A heavy scent of perfume filled the air.

Her mother hovered over the children. "This is the worst they've been in a long time," she said. "My daughter's a single mother, don't you know. She doesn't get a dime from their father and he never comes to see the boys either. Good riddance, I say." She sat on a chair near my desk. Every now and then she had a choking cough. She looked toward me apologetically. "I should know better. I can't stop smoking . . . hard as I try. It's murder on me and I know it's bad for them."

The older woman held one of the children on her lap. She stroked his hair and planted a noisy kiss on his cheek. There was no scent of cologne but rather a sick smell of sweat and stale tobacco clinging to her overweight body.

They were nearly ready to leave. I scribbled a list of instructions for the children's care and made arrangements for nebulizing equipment for home use. Hazel was near the exam table and I watched with some surprise when she picked up my tape measure. She encircled her waist and purred with glee as she read the numbers.

"Listen," I said. "I want you to call me if there is any change in the older one's breathing. You have a prescription for prednisone, but unless he improves quickly he may need to be put in the hospital."

Grandma nodded her head in agreement. Hazel had a vacant stare.

"Do you have any questions?" I asked.

She moved toward the door. "Yes," she said and pointed toward the scale in the hall. "Do you mind if I weigh myself. I hope I haven't gained too much."

They marched out of the office. So much for the maternal instinct.

CHAPTER 25

✍

Sammy's Sad Song

Sammy stood before the full length mirror, stark naked. He clicked the bolt shut and felt secure in his privacy. There were a few bits of fuzz on his upper lip and he was pleased to see some stray shoots of hair on his chest. Some of the fellows in his class had started to shave over a year ago. Perhaps the few inches in height that he had added during the summer and the growth of his penis and testicles meant he was a mature adult. He marked his height with a pencil on the wall chart and jotted down his early morning weight also. He reached for his bathrobe and turned on the stereo.

Sammy's mother's knock interrupted his musing.

"You're wanted on the phone," she called. "You didn't hear me, Sammy. Is everything all right? I mean, the door's locked and you've been upstairs for hours. It's not like you."

"Everything's fine. I was just listening to my tapes and didn't want to be bothered. Jill likes to butt in and mess my stuff up, so I thought I'd make sure she kept out."

"She's at her friend's house. She'll be sleeping over tonight so you won't have to worry. Now get the phone and then come down for supper."

Sammy' conversation was brief. He arranged a tennis match for the next afternoon and went upstairs to finish dressing. As he was pulling his T-shirt over his head, he felt a firm prominence on the right side of his chest. He threw his T-shirt on the bed and went back to the mirror. The swelling involved the breast and it was something he had never noticed before. There was a good-sized disc around the nipple area and he was able to wiggle the tissue back and forth. He found nothing like it on the other side.

What could it be? Who could he tell? He certainly wouldn't dare strip in the shower after gym and have the guys think he was a girl. Was he growing a teat? He'd be the joke of the year.

Sammy was silent at dinner. His father was puzzled when he passed up dessert and asked to be excused. Pecan pie. His son's leading choice, and he didn't want a nibble.

"What's happening?" he asked his wife. "What do you make of Sammy skipping dessert? Did he feel all right this morning? You know, he did look a little peaked. Should I go up to him?"

"A little later. Let him be alone for now."

Sammy sat at his desk with a blank sheet of paper in front of him. He buried his head in his hands and began to cry. For three or four minutes he remained a statue, and then he dried his tears, slipped the paper into the typewriter and hammered out a few lines.

He turned off the light and extended himself on the bed. He couldn't dodge the inevitable. If the swelling of the breast was still there later in the week, he'd have to ask his parents to have the doctor examine him.

He wasn't able to concentrate on the lyrics of his favorite song, and after flipping the pages of the *Sporting News* without interest, he got up, sealed the envelope with his typed message, and went downstairs to be with his family.

"I didn't mean to be a pain," he said. "Just wasn't hungry. Maybe I got the bug or something."

"Yeah," his father added. "I thought you looked a little washed out. I told your mother. Get to bed early tonight. If you don't feel better in the morning, you ought to stay home."

Sammy agreed. "Some extra sleep'll fix me up. I don't want to get behind now. We've got our first test in chemistry this week and they pile on homework."

He went to school the next day. At his mother's insistence he swallowed a piece of toast and washed it down with a half of a glass of orange juice. He went to the nurse's office after the first period and had her take his temperature. It was normal, but she advised him to forget gym and swimming practice. When school was over he walked to his friend's house, cancelled his tennis date and hurried home.

He couldn't wait out the week. The breast was still a worrisome, frightening part of his maturing body. It wasn't as it should be.

Sammy was as forlorn as any teenager I had ever seen. His size eleven shoes stretched over the end of the examining table. He gave me a poor excuse for a smile when I walked in.

"Do you mind if my mother waits in the other room?" he asked.

"Of course not. You're old enough to be here by yourself, just not old enough to drive. She can read one of my magazines; they've probably been here for years. Maybe there's some stories she hasn't seen."

Sammy's palms were sweaty. His pulse was racing, and he let out several deep sighs.

"Doctor," he began, "I've got to show you something. It's not normal. I know that much. It's been there going on a week. Maybe more. I noticed it when I finished my shower."

"Slow down," I said. "Let's see what you've discovered. And did you tell your folks you were upset or did you say you wanted to have yourself looked at?"

"I didn't want them to worry. That's why I asked my mom to leave."

"Go on."

"I've got this thing on my chest. Right around my nipple. Geez, Doctor . . ." He lifted his shirt and touched the spot gingerly.

"That?" I broke out laughing. His face grew rosy red.

"Sammy," I said, "get off the table and get dressed. Don't waste your time and mine. Half the fellows your age have that little ring of tissue when they start to grow. It's absolutely nothing. It's a hormone your body makes when your glands begin to act up."

"And," I added, "it'll go away within the year . . . may occur on the other side also, but it's not anything dangerous."

"You're sure?"

"Positive."

"Will you call my mother in?"

"Mom," Sammy said exultantly, "take that envelope out of your purse. That's it. Now, please tear it up in shreds. I don't need it after all."

She took out the envelope, tore it in little pieces and handed it to him.

"Will you let me in on the mystery?" I asked.

Sammy boomed an answer.

"That was my will, Doctor."

"How come?"

"I was sure I had cancer . . . or was some kind of freak . . . you know, with teats growing. If I had cancer, it would be quick at my age. I wanted my sister to get my stereo, my cousin my ten-speed, but since I'll be around, who needs a will?"

CHAPTER 26

❧

Candy and Canes

Two itches, more than ten years apart, were pieces of an interesting puzzle. I met Al for the first time aboard ship and we became fast friends. It turned out that he was the only serviceman from my home town on our attack transport, and a closeness grew between us. We found many mutual interests, went on liberty together, shopped for souvenirs in the strange ports of the Orient, drank in the magic of their civilization. We knew we never would have wandered through the crowded streets gathering bits and pieces of a different culture if there had been no war. We agreed that we should plan to meet regularly after discharge and reminisce. It was that kind of a friendship.

We were sidetracked when the war ended. Al went back to college to get his M.B.A. and I opened my pediatric office. Al was an orthodox Jew who followed all the rituals of his religion. He kept a kosher kitchen, went to Friday night services and faithfully observed all the major holidays. He never rode to temple, no matter how blustery the weather, figuring a walk through snow or rain was one of the inconveniences of adhering to his beliefs.

Before discharge, we had gone hunting for souvenirs of our Pacific adventures. I had just learned that I was the father of a little girl and so I dragged Al though countless shops in Kowloon, China, while I selected a suitable silk dress for my new daughter.

As I paid for my purchases, Al spied a row of canes in a display case. He was ecstatic. He yelled to me.

"Hey, Doc, hold it, will you? Look at these beauties. Just right for my grandfather. I'll bring him a fancy cane or a walking stick for the holidays. A stick from China! He'll get a charge out of that."

Al inspected every cane in the store. He finally settled for one that was heavy and highly polished with distinctive ornamental markings. There would be nothing like this back home.

"Feel the heft of this," Al said. "It'll last forever."

We walked to the dock and waited for our ride back to the ship. Each of us was excited about presenting our gift when we returned home. Back on board, I took the red dress out of the package a dozen times and admired the fine needlework and ran my fingers over the soft material. Laura Jean would be a smash hit in this exotic dress.

Al rushed to prepare his gear for the trip home, too. He loaded everything into his sea chest, wrapped the lacquered cane in several towels and put it on top of the heap. He shipped it home the same day and expected to follow later in the week.

Just before midnight, Al burst into my stateroom. His eyes were swollen shut, his cheeks and lips were puffy and misshapen. He could hardly talk.

"Doc, Doc, what the hell's happening to me?" he croaked. "I'm covered with a goddam rash. Everyplace!"

His body was a collection of welts. Small wonder he was so upset.

"I itch like mad, and it's driving me nuts. What can it be?"

"You're allergic to something, Al. That's obvious. I'll give you a new medicine . . . it's potent and it works fast. I'll admit you to sick bay tonight to make sure you don't have trouble with your breathing. If that happens, I'll be able to treat you with adrenalin. It'll clear you up . . . there's not much chance you'll be bothered in that way, but let's play it safe."

We went over everything we could think of. No new foods; we hadn't eaten anything while we were ashore. No medicines other than atabrine, and he had taken that for months. There were no bites anywhere that I could find. I told him it wasn't a venereal disease and that he'd be able to go home on time if the swelling went down. We'd have to figure out what caused the allergic reaction, though, or it could happen again and again.

Al's skin cleared within a day and he left for civilian life. I didn't hear from him for several years. Just a letter, letting me know he had enrolled in college under the GI Bill. He added a postscript. He'd given his grandfather the lacquered cane in time for Rosh Hashonah, the Jewish New Year. But Al developed another case of hives; more severe this time and it pointed to the cane as the villain. It was the lacquered cane.

I found out that lacquer is made from tree resins and contains uroshiol, a toxic irritant that is found in the poison ivy plant as well. He must have been sensitized to this group of resins many years ago and handling his grandfather's gift created the allergic response.

My office nurse saw David sitting morosely in the waiting room. His face was blown up as round as a pumpkin. His eyes were narrow slits and he was digging at his abdomen furiously. The nurse took pity on the young child and called me away from my more pedestrian cases.

His mother was crying. She pointed to David. "I found him like this when he got up from his nap. It's crazy. Every time I look there's another part of him that's got those bumps."

Elena grabbed my hand as she asked me, "This isn't one of those awful new diseases, is it? I've seen so many specials on TV. You never know what to expect next. I'm nearly out of my mind."

"No, no, nothing like that," I reassured her. "David will be all right, Elena. He has giant urticaria. That means in everyday terms, big hives. He's allergic to something."

"Allergic? Oh, that's all, huh?"

"Yep." I began to chuckle. "This takes me back a lot of years. When Al and I were in the Navy. Like father, like son; you know how it goes. Especially with allergies."

She relaxed a little. "Al's told me that story a hundred times. But, Doctor, his grandfather's been dead for years. Who knows what became of that cane? The one he shipped from China."

I looked at the boy. "David, you'll be fine. I'll give you one day for these things to go away. That's all. Then back to school. You're in Pre-K, aren't you?"

David held on to his Teddy bear. He was a forlorn little boy who looked as if a swarm of bees had attacked him.

"Uh, huh," was all he would say.

Elena stood protectively next to her son.

"Doctor, Davey's hard to give medicine. He spits everything out. Can you give him a shot instead? Would you believe he'd take that over swallowing medicine?"

I stared at the child in disbelief but gave him the antihistamine injection.

"Let's review a few facts while we're waiting," I said. "At Davey's age, foods cause giant hives most often. Special things. Seafoods, chocolate, nuts, things like that for starters."

Elena thought a minute, then said, "He hasn't had anything new at home but, you know, both Al and I have parents in town. The Jewish parents and the Irish ones. They take turns spoiling him. Let's see, my folks have the same menu every weekend. Nothing very fancy. Fish on

Friday, stew on Saturday and he's back home on Sunday."

"What about treats; cookies with coconut and so on?"

"He gets a lot of that. But it's apple pie or vanilla ice cream at Mom and Dad's."

"And at Al's."

She laughed. "They're really programmed. Friday night meals—gefilte fish, chicken soup, challah, roast meat and then sponge cake. I had that every time I went there. On Saturday, chicken was the main dish, with roast potatoes and tzimmes. The dessert—always ices."

"That gives me something to work on, Elena," I said. "This kid's got a great thing going for him. Special attention from both sides. Where was he yesterday? Whose weekend was it?"

"Al's parents."

"Let's check the patient. The brave guy who doesn't mind shots."

"Doctor, it's magic. He looks better already."

"He does, doesn't he? He won't have to stick around much longer. But you'll have to coax him to take some medicine by mouth or he'll have to come back for another pinch in the arm."

I rummaged around in my desk drawer for a sticker to give Davey. Children that age treasure stamps that proclaim their bravery.

"What do you have in your pockets?" I asked him. "Do you have a place for all these stickers?"

He hurried to make room for his award. He pulled a half-eaten candy bar from his blue denim jacket and dropped it on my desk.

"Hm, halvah—from Al's folk's house, I suppose."

I read the ingredients to Elena. "Chocolate, cane sugar, sesame oil. Bet you it's the sesame oil. We'd better stay away from imports for both of your boys."

I pulled the dictionary from the shelf.

"According to this . . . halvah . . . a Turkish confection consisting of a paste made of ground sesame seeds and nuts mixed with honey."

I turned a few pages . . . "Lacquer—any of various resinous varnishes, especially a natural varnish obtained from a Japanese tree, *Rhus verniciflua*, used to produce a highly polished, lustrous surface on wood, etc."

The voice of my receptionist came over the intercom. "Doctor, Davey's father is in the waiting room. Should I send him in?"

"Sure. His family's about ready to leave. Why doesn't he come in and say hello?"

Al was a little heavier than in the old days but otherwise unchanged. He picked his son up, hoisted him over his shoulders, took Elena by the hand and started to the door. After all the time we had spent together, there wasn't a lot we had in common, other than an interest in Davey's welfare. Those promises for regular reunions were casualties of our busy schedules.

"It's quite a coincidence, Elena," I said. "Davey and Al are very allergic people. Different causes but the same kind of skin reactions. I've seen lots of families where almost everyone sneezes during ragweed season or wheezes when they are near animals. But these fellows are in a class by themselves."

Al grinned as he was leaving my office. "Just wanted to keep you on your toes, Doc. Nothing like an itchy rash to make you scrounge around for the answer."

CHAPTER 27

❦

Father Gabriel

My wife and I sat in the back row of the cathedral. The ceremony was overpowering. The enraptured look on all the faces made this ordination unforgettable. It was not my religion, not my house of worship, but it was easy to be carried away by the service.

The young man stood before the congregation at this time of sanctification, ready to assume his priesthood. He was about to fulfill a pledge made many years before—in a hospital room, with a much different audience observing him.

At that time his mother and father were at his side, waiting for him to awaken from a prolonged coma. He was in a short hospital gown, with ties in the back, nearly hidden under the oxygen canopy. His arms were immobile at his sides. The steady drip, drip of IV glucose carried energy throughout his body.

For twenty days I had observed the same scene. An unconscious youth in a state of hibernation; no clue that he would ever emerge. His parents were part of the scenery of the bleak room. When I made my daily rounds, they'd search for a sign that he had improved; failing to sense a change, they'd return to keep their vigil.

He had never convulsed before this illness. They had heard a cry and then a crash as he hit the hardwood floor. Jerky movements of his arms, tightly clenched jaws, heavy breathing and deep stupor; as if all connection to the world had been cut, the master switch turned off. When I reached their home, he was no longer having fits. He did not respond to any stimuli, painful or otherwise. Then he began to twitch again, a series of violent muscle contractions involving his whole body. They could not be controlled with the medications in my bag, and it took large amounts of barbiturates in the emergency room before the agitations ended.

We ran test after test on his spinal fluid and his blood and sent specimens to the state research laboratory before the diagnosis of equine encephalitis could be proven. We theorized that he must have been bitten by a mosquito carrying the virus while he was playing in the marshy fields near his home. That was the diagnosis I presented to the parents, but I couldn't provide any treatment. There was no effective therapy for this nervous system infection. We could just maintain some level of nutrition either by tube or vein, and sedate him so he wouldn't convulse again, and wait.

We called in some infectious disease experts who tapped his knees, looked at his pupils, studied the brain waves and turned away when they acknowledged it was encephalitis. They reiterated the uncertain prognosis for the young patient.

"Have you given up too, Doctor?" his father asked me as the weeks passed.

"I haven't given up," I said. "It's just that I realize nothing's changing. He doesn't react. He's the way he was the day he took sick."

"Everything hasn't been tried," the man said quietly. "We haven't given prayer a chance. It's not hopeless, you know. We have faith and we know he's going to get better."

"I'd be the last one to argue against that."

Miracles aren't always instantaneous. But a flicker of an eyelid one day; then a movement of his hand. A process of rebirth almost. A groan of distress was greeted as if the veil was being lifted, and he was reaching out to the world again. Inch by inch he left his hibernation. The pace of recovery accelerated. He was able to sit and feed himself, to talk and at least take a few wobbly steps down the hall.

I began to discuss rehabilitation and arranged for the next weeks to be spent at home. A physiotherapist was engaged to stop by and help him exercise his weakened muscles.

He was in a wheelchair the day he went home. His father turned to me as his son left the hospital room.

"Doctor, you're invited to his ordination." There was a huge smile on his face. He piled the mass of cards from his son's classmates into a suitcase and placed them on the boy's lap. "It'll be a few years, of course, but we'll remind you when the time comes."

"Thanks a lot," I said. "Even though I don't know what you're talking about."

"I know you don't. When I said that we were going to pray he'd wake up and be himself again, we made a promise. He would give his life to serve, to be a priest. You'll see, it will happen."

I wouldn't question this decision though it was not made by the boy. The story of Abraham and Isaac was being replayed and faith was as strong as in biblical days.

They sent me an invitation, as they said they would. Their son, Father Gabriel, was to be ordained.

CHAPTER 28

❧

The Incidence of Coincidence

We were sitting at a table in a Florida pancake parlor. My colleague, Stewie, had retired from his busy Ob/Gyn practice several years earlier. It was traditional for us to meet once a year and reminisce about the past. Although our wives had shared the stress of practice with us, they had a different version of the glory of our profession.

The conversation was spirited as we relaxed in the busy, high calorie junk food eatery. The discussion was a scientific analysis of our menu choices. Forget the cholesterol or remember our arteries was the greatest issue before us when our waitress appeared.

She was a trim woman in her late 50's. Her greying hair was neatly in place and her uniform was crisp and spotless. She reached into her pocket for a pen and then let out a loud "Oh, my God!"

To the utter consternation of our wives she raced over and threw her arms around my friend and planted a noisy kiss on his forehead. She then turned to me and treated me similarly.

"What a surprise! What a surprise!" she kept repeating.

Finally turning toward the startled spectators in the restaurant she explained, "These two men were my doctors. The cute white-haired one . . . he delivered all of my children," she said, pointing to my old associate. "And this man was the pediatrician."

Stewie and I regained our composure and looked at the excited woman. He smiled and remarked, "Tammy Barnes. She's still surprising me—just the way she did back home. She made the headlines," he reminded our wives. "This lady was a candidate for the Guiness Book of Records. No kidding. It was amazing. I never ran into anything like it, never."

It had quieted down in the restaurant and our waitress was ready for our order. We figured we needed extra energy after all the excitement of the doctor/patient reunion and we ordered the specialty of the house.

We were served coffee while the kitchen prepared the gigantic, loaded-with-everything, apple pancakes. Stewie plunged into a review of the wondrous pregnancies of Tammy, our waitress. I waited to add my bit.

"Tammy Barnes," Stewie said. "That name fit pretty well when she was a young kid waiting for her first, but later it should have been something like . . . like Mother Earth."

"She was waiting on tables in a small place in town when she took a leave of absence for her first baby. She was sixteen years old or so, married and all that and her pregnancy was a breeze."

He went on. "She went back to work, then had another kid, then one more. Her husband didn't earn much so she put in as many overtime hours as possible; banquets, wedding receptions and the lot. Somehow they managed. What with the two of them pitching in . . . working together. Until the first big crisis. Lots of people have lots of babies. One at a time. But she was much larger with her fourth pregnancy because she was having triplets. What a shock for them, trying to get by with the ones they already had."

Our puffy pancakes were placed in front of us and we dug in. The waitress plied us with more coffee and confided that she could hardly wait to tell her children and grandchildren about today's meeting. She had been in Florida for more than fifteen years and now she was a widow who was not looking for another man. Just some peace and quiet and a place to put her feet up and relax.

We finished our delicacies and our wives waited for more of Stewie's story. He was happy to oblige.

"The triplets were pretty good sized and our friend managed O.K. The babies had to stay in the hospital a little longer. Fred'll tell you about that. But they weren't more than one year old and she was back carting trays at the big hotel."

I added some observations. "When those triplets came in to see me, they took over my office. Everybody was bowled over by them. They gaped at the three whirlwinds and were grateful they didn't have to feed them, dress them, chase after them and all that. The other parents were too embarrassed to complain about diaper rashes or pinworms after seeing what she had to endure."

Stewie turned to his wife and said, "You know what's coming next. It comes back to you, doesn't it? The unbelievable part."

She nodded. "Of course. How could I forget? You didn't talk about anything else for weeks. The reporters kept calling, even one of the TV channels wanted to know about your patient."

"Yeah, we were celebrities for a little while, I guess. The triplets were three years old when she came to see me. I never saw anyone who was larger with child—remember that euphemism for pregnancy—when she was in her seventh month. She was burdened with a real load. Her legs were swollen and she waddled into the examining room and showed me her varicose veins . . . bulged out like purple pipes. And her stretch marks looked like the Grand Canyon."

He looked over at our waitress. She was carrying the dirty dishes from another table back to the kitchen. Quite slim now . . . such a small woman to be able to carry triplets.

"When I realized that she was having another threesome, I couldn't believe the statistical probability that anyone could have two sets in a row. The law of averages puts that random chance into the record books."

"My part began again when these miracles were delivered," I said. "They were smaller than the first batch. We had plenty of help in the delivery room that day and it came in handy. All girls with squashed little noses, heads out of shape a little from being pushed out. They needed to be suctioned and stimulated and warmed before they began to cry and stir around."

I looked over to my wife and teased her a bit. "You always liked those wildlife specials on TV. But babies aren't anything like that. They don't get up on spindly legs, fall down like a collapsing card table and get up again. They don't weave in a drunken trot over to their mothers and start to nurse."

She gave me a "there you go again" kind of look and I went on.

"Finally all the worries during their first week were over and they stayed in the nursery for the better part of a month. It took that long for them to suck well enough to gain some weight."

The celebrated mother approached our table. "Can I get you anything else?" she asked.

I patted my stomach.

"No way I could hold another drop. But could you sit down a minute with us? Do you think the manager would mind? I was telling our wives how it was when you took your babies home. The second ones."

She beamed. The demure little waitress reached for a chair and pulled it alongside.

"The hell with him," she laughed. "I've been on my feet in this business for over forty years. If I want to sit down with my guests, that's my choice. Let him fire me."

"Great."

She listened intently as I went on. "They'd been home a couple of weeks and it was time for me to stop over and check up on them. They were expecting me and when I rang the bell one of the neighbors let me in. We went up to their big bedroom upstairs."

Her eyes glistened and she described the way they had set up the nursery. Diapers were piled in stacks, folded, snowy white ready for the many changes; shirts and booties and nightgowns with the drawstring sleeves; cotton balls and baby lotion and powder for their bottoms; bibs and burp cloths; three rockers—one for each alongside the bassinets. Tammy giggled as she talked about feeding times during those early days. They had to be fed in shifts when she was lucky enough to have some helpers. When she did, each baby would be snuggled and fed while being rocked ever so gently.

And the bottles. "I sometimes still see them in my dreams," she said. "Racks of bottles were in one of those little refrigerators. And on the big dressing tables we had three or four bottle warmers to take the chill out of the formula."

I took over and recalled the scene at that home visit. There were some volunteers at first. Some of them helped care for the other children . . . the older triplets weren't in school yet and they had to be watched all the time.

Tammy heaped praise on her neighbors for rescuing her from certain insanity. They pitched in and did the cooking, cleaning and the endless laundry as well as spelling her off some nights during those feeding sessions.

The scene might have seemed chaotic but the family got through the years of raising all those children and were lost to both Stewie and me.

Here we were thousands of miles from where it all started . . . sitting in a restaurant sharing glimpses into the wonderful scrapbook of Tammy Barnes' life.

CHAPTER 29

✦

Franklin

Franklin's life took an early detour. It was the custom to circumcise all newborn boys at the regional hospital where he was born, but the routine procedure had an unexpected complication. Franklin's surgical wound wouldn't stop bleeding. A frantic hour was spent trying to control the oozing. The tube of blood drawn for cross-matching with the donor wouldn't clot. Franklin was a hemophiliac.

Our paths crossed for the first time during my residency training days when he was hurried into the emergency room with a gash on his knee. The treatment was rather routine for Franklin. He was only in third grade but had already visited the clinic enough times to have a weighty dossier. He was such a wild kid that his behavior made our efforts futile.

I remember my first meeting and how I chuckled when he described his accident. He knew that he was at the center of this particular stage and he played the emergency room audience to the hilt.

"I didn't start it," he began. "We were playing ball in the yard. He'd been buggin' me . . . calling me names and all that. Sissy, coward, cripple . . . you know. Got me real mad."

I listened to his recital and held an ice bag to his swollen knee. "Why was he picking on you? Had you guys had trouble before?" I asked.

"Sure," he said. "The creep always made fun of me. He knew I had to wear a helmet whenever we went out on the field. The other kids never said nothin'. Just Billy. Oh, how I hated him!"

Franklin's right knee was scraped and bruised, but the ominous swelling meant that blood was filling the joint space. The lab was setting up for a pint of blood. A look at his chart was a reminder that a transfusion was the only way we could control his bleeding.

"What happened after that?"

His eyes sparkled and he shouted, "What happened? I got even. Boy, did I get even!"

"Calm down, honey." Franklin's mother had been listening to her son's report of the schoolyard accident. She squeezed his hand reassuredly. "The doctor will fix you up as good as new and we'll go home."

"Yeah, I know. But Mom I want to let him hear what happened." He went on. "The jerk was playing second base and I was at bat. He was still yelling all those things at me. I nearly got hit with the first pitch, but bang! —the next one was right over the plate and I smacked it over his head."

He winced as we flexed his knee gently. Then he continued. "I went round first base and headed for second. Johnny, he's an outfielder, threw the ball to Billy and he was waiting to tag me."

Another pause and then the finale. He gave me a big grin and erupted. "Did I ever bowl him over. I slid right into that sucker and the ball popped out of his mitt. So I hurt my knee . . . but I was safe!"

He seemed hopeless. Perhaps he had developed a fatalistic attitude at his young age. He knew the ice packs and the transfusions wouldn't cure his clotting defect.

His mother and I talked about his swashbuckling behavior and she too felt that he was defying the gods that had dictated he would have the menace of bleeding hovering over him.

There was progress in research over the years. Franklin no longer needed to spend hours in the outpatient department watching blood drip slowly from a plastic bag. Instead new plasma products, first cryoprecipitate and then Factor VIII concentrate reached the market. These substances raised the clotting capacity of the blood and could be administered at home. His mother found that she had a delicate touch and once she overcame her squeamishness, was quite an expert.

Franklin outgrew pediatric caregivers and I lost track of him. I learned from some of his friends that he no longer had his daredevil approach to life. His knees and ankles had become stiff and immobile from his early injuries and he turned his energy in other directions.

Some years later he appeared at my office with a pregnant young woman at his side. He sat across the desk from me after finding a comfortable chair for his wife.

"Remember me, Doctor?" He gave me a big smile. "I'm Franklin. My wife and I are here for a prenatal visit."

"How could I forget you? You're about to become a father! And you have decided that you'd forgive me for all the terrible things I did to you when you were growing up."

I turned to his wife and asked her the usual questions about her pregnancy; the due date and her own health history. She was a stunning looking young woman, flushed with the glow that sometimes comes with expectancy. She was easy to talk to and the two young people held hands tightly as we discussed this exciting part of their lives.

She mentioned her expected date and told me that she had had an easy time of it so far. She had been told all about hemophilia and how it was transmitted, so her mind was at ease. The female is the carrier; the males are the patients. There were a great many unrelated questions that occupied her mind and I was able to answer them readily.

Franklin and I were able to bring each other up to date. He had finished school and went to work in a dead-end kind of job. He spent a few years traveling, just marking time, then returned to college and surprised himself and his family with his academic performance.

"Would you have guessed, Doctor, that I graduated and am a bona-fide, honest-to-goodness, computer engineer? That I have a great job and Judy and I work for the same company. He reached for her hand. "We both want you to take care of our baby. How about it?" Then he added, "My mother sends her best and hopes that you'll be her grandchild's doctor."

I shook hands with them "I'm awfully glad you came to see me. It's a bright spot in my day."

The heartaches that were to face this young couple could not have been anticipated. The discovery of the blood products that simplified Franklin's care allowed a mysterious virus to wreak havoc on his immune system.

The Factor VIII concentrate that raises the level in hemophiliacs is obtained from a large pool of donors. Many of the donors are drifters who jump at the chance of a few extra dollars in exchange for a pint of their blood. Thousands of units of this processed, pooled material were transfused before it was discovered that AIDS, as well as hepatitis, could be spread along with the blessed anti-hemophiliac factor.

Somewhere in Franklin's years of struggle he received a batch of the new plague-like virus and he became another statistic. He was among the four to five percent who acquired HIV without high-risk behavior.

Judy and Franklin were thrilled with their son. It wasn't until he was three months old and his stubborn thrush wouldn't resolve that we discovered the truth. His poor growth, as well as the yeast infection that clung to his mucous membrane and skin, was caused by AIDS. Testing of Judy proved that she had received this killer germ from Franklin.

The treatment available to overcome HIV infections was not curative and seldom slowed the relentless course of the disease. I became another passive observer as these vital people fought to live.

All that could be done was to try to combat the destruction of their immune system and attempt to ease their suffering. The irony of getting through the early years only to be felled by a rogue micro-organism. The inevitable dissolution of this family was tragic and our impotence in curing the infection was reason for despair.

What has been conquered, I thought, if we solve one problem only to replace it with something more menacing?

CHAPTER 30

❧

A Special Family

Some people shake their fists and curse fate when adversity appears. Not Harold and Joanne. They were expecting their first child after many years of marriage. Excitement spilled over into every corner of their lives. They whispered to each other far into the night, planning for the arrival and discussing how their lives would be enriched.

Harold even tagged along when Joanne visited the obstetrician. He sat in the waiting room and smiled at the expectant mothers and found that some weren't at all jubilant over the pregnancy and there were those who were as bubbly as his wife.

They followed the doctor's directions religiously. Harold accompanied Joanne when she walked the prescribed two-mile walk their physician suggested. It seemed to him as rigorous as the Boston Marathon but it was on the list of things to do. Each morning he weighed himself on the bathroom scale and charted his numbers next to hers. Her weight crept up gradually and he was delighted when he shed a few pounds.

When she felt life and guided his hand to her abdomen, their exultation was unequalled. The little fluttering, quivering movements were like the discovery of a new planet. It was a memorable day in their lives. The growing wonder of it all was capped when the sonogram projected the image of form and substance to their dream.

Joanne was radiant. This was her greatest adventure. The monotony of her job and its limited future would be replaced by a different role. She would have their baby to care for and there would be a new dimension to her life.

Harold's work at the post office was enough to provide for them and, if necessary, he would moonlight for the extras that he wanted their child to have.

Harold was a balding, round-faced man with a cherubic appearance. His unlined face reflected his quiet disposition. He found everything about the state of expectancy fascinating. He quit his weekly poker group and spent his time stripping wallpaper from the alcove next to their bed-room and painting and decorating it for the tenant soon to arrive. The crib from his parent's attic was sanded and refinished with lead-free paint. Decals were pasted on the walls and teddy bears and music boxes were gobbled up at garage sales and sanitized for the nursery.

He even gave up his cigars. No polluted air in their house . . . never, never was his pledge.

The delivery was easy. Harold and Joanne saw the shock of black hair, the round cheeks and blue eyes and they were contented. The baby was a handsome replica of his father. He just needed bifocal glasses and a couple hundred more pounds and they'd be twins.

No one has ever been able to explain why Phillip didn't fulfill the idyllic dream. He remained the same as the months went by. A child in his crib looking momentarily at his hands, then his eyes would dart away, never focusing on faces or noticing the objects in the nursery. He would just lie quietly mewing little sounds, always in his private world.

Joanne rocked him to sleep with soft melodies. She sang to him and tried to bring him in touch with the love and hope that filled her heart.

Phillip's body grew just the way the average infant's did. But as the certainty that his progress was not normal struck home, they didn't change their routine. Harold talked to his son, told him stories, wheeled him in the park, sat at his bedside dry-eyed. Their baby was still a miracle to them. There was no reason to cry.

I admired their acceptance that Phillip would not achieve the goals that most parents seek for their children. He was their gift to each other and their sorrow, if it was present, never surfaced.

Phillip's features were flawless. He was a beautiful little boy discon-nected somehow from the rest of us. He didn't seem to notice his parents' presence. All of his needs were met. He was fed and diapered and was never alone but he was always alone.

There were some illnesses that threatened his survival but he weath-ered them all and yet his hibernation persisted.

A new routine was established. The interests of both parents centered around their son. Harold would carry Phillip into my office and fill my ears with the amazing feats of his son.

"I was telling Phillip just the other day about my new job at work," he might say. "I told him that I'd have an extra day off and we'd spend it together."

I would nod and Joanne would recite her observations abut her curly-haired boy.

"He likes to sit near the window and look out at the other children. He loves to have them ring the bell and come and visit with us. There are cookies near his bed and he always shares them with his friends."

They went along with this harmless charade. Harold made a ritual of sitting with Phillip every evening after work. He told his son the stories he remembered from his own childhood and then new original tales were created. Somehow the telling of the magic of youth helped him deal with his son's empty life.

When I learned of Harold's storytelling skills, I asked him to record these fantasies . . . his fairy tales. Perhaps they could be used to entertain other children who were isolated from their peers by their own plight.

He grasped the challenge and some wonderful tapes found their way to my office. His world of make-believe was warm and safe. Of course there were happy endings and the children were comforted by the stories.

Harold's caring nature wasn't confined to his child. He volunteered each year to be Santa Claus and the children who climbed on his knee heard tall tales, and he promised them their wishes would come true.

One day Harold came to see me. He was alone. He carried a large box filled with books. There were dozens of thin volumes to be distributed to my patients. He had written a Santa Claus story for his handicapped son and had it illustrated and printed by a local publisher.

It was a gift, he said, from Phillip to be shared by other children during the holiday season. He sat in my waiting room one busy afternoon and watched with delight as the nurse gave each child Phillip's present.

CHAPTER 31

❧

The Juice of the Watermelon

Sal didn't know he was the "significant other" in Annie Mae's life. He wouldn't have cared anyway. They were common-law mates, welded firmly by the bonds of their commitment. Their union was stronger than ever after thirty-nine years of being together.

He was a small, fifty-year-old man with curly hair, untouched as yet by streaks of grey. His straight nose, deep black eyes, strong chin and old-fashioned handlebar mustache gave him an attractive appearance. His slight frame allowed him to slip into the ditches that he dug. Ditches, cellar foundations, anything that needed a pick and shovel, were handled expertly by Sal. Six days a week he'd report to the contractor, hear the assignment and start to burrow. Steadily from the first shovelful, the dirt would fly. No stopping for coffee breaks or one of his beloved cigars. The elements couldn't beat him. A plugged sewer line from a summer flood or a frozen pipe in subzero weather were obstacles that had to be tackled. He was a reliable troubleshooter from the old country. Sal couldn't read or write, but the engineers ignored their blueprints and collared him for practical judgments. Could they fit a three-inch pipe in that area or did he think there'd be enough pitch for drainage?

He learned to pace himself. He would pull his watch from his pocket, press the stem of the old, gold heirloom, look at the hands and climb out of the ditch. He'd lay his tools near the mountain of dirt and wash up for lunch.

His Annie Mae seldom varied the menu. Two sandwiches, a pickle or a tomato, a hunk of cake or a piece of pie and a thermos of coffee. The meal would be downed methodically. Sal would then lean against a tree trunk, light up a little cigarillo and let his muscles rest. He'd sit, like a gladiator between bouts, summoning up energy for the next encounter.

His short respite finished, Sal would snuff out his cigar, put his lunch pail in the cab of his pick-up truck, check the time and begin to dig again. His rest period was over in a half an hour, union or no union.

146

Annie Mae didn't have the strength to do much around the house. She suffered from female trouble, she told anyone who would listen, and she couldn't do any heavy lifting. She had a hernia that had given her trouble ever since the last surgery and there was a tumor bigger than a grapefruit that had to come out. But the doctors warned her that unless she rested more and built up her blood, she might not live through the surgery. She was told that she "had sugar" and she was dizzy when she was out of bed too long.

She reminded Sal that she was worn out. Her pregnancies had been miserable. They had to hire a lady to stay with her for weeks before Famia was born and God knows how she survived without help when little Anthony came along.

Annie Mae had watery blue eyes that looked faded. A round face, a number of chins that descended in steps down to the base of her neck. Her enormous body was always clothed in a light blue nightgown. She'd dress for church on Sunday, but then would take to her bed right after the noon meal. Sal and the children had to manage after that.

He loved her. He paid the doctor bills without complaint. He shopped for groceries, bought the children's clothes, went alone to parents' night. He coaxed the children to study and tried to grasp some of the puzzles of grammar along with them.

When he'd sit at Annie Mae's bedside, he'd pour out his heart to her. There was no mention of the hours of physical labor or the frost-bitten fingers or the shooting pain that radiated down the back of his thigh when he lifted buckets of dirt from a construction trench.

"Five more payments and we own this place. Remember when you said we could never afford three bedrooms, a parlor, a porch and a gas furnace. Remember?"

She smiled. "I remember. How about when the roof leaked the year after we moved in and you and your brother fixed it? You who was so scared of ladders?"

Sal laughed. "If only you'd feel better, Annie Mae," he said. "That's all I want. We got everything we need. Just want you to be better."

"I bet that Dr. Howley can help. He's that new specialist, Sal. I heard he has wonderful ways to cure people. Really. He has a machine that melts tumors, even as big as mine. Don't need no surgery."

Sal took her plump, white hand and pressed it in his. "Go see him. Call him tomorrow. Don't wait."

Annie Mae sighed, "He's expensive, Sal. It don't come cheap. And they say you have to pay in advance or he can't be bothered. Maybe I'll forget it. I'll see what our own doctor can do."

"No, we won't. We'll get the money. Let me worry about that. Annie Mae, who told you about this specialist? Where's his office?"

"Mrs. Sweet. A lady you worked for last fall. She had a leaky basement. It got flooded after the big storm. She told me."

"Mrs. Sweet? But she wasn't sick. Her boy was. Said he had sugar. Like you."

"You musta said something about me, Sal, when you were working there, 'cause she called last week. All excited that Ronnie, her son, was gettin' better. Then she said this Dr. Howley had fixed him up, and she was sure he could do something for me. Even for that growth of mine."

"That's funny. She was taking him to Famia and Tony's doctor. He was great with our kids. With the croup and when Tony got knocked out."

"Sal, our doctor's good with kids. But this man didn't need no shots to clear up her boy's sugar."

Ronnie Sweet had been referred to me by his family physician. He was a ten-year-old whose personality appealed to everyone but his self-pitying mother. He was a bed-wetter who exhausted his mother's patience. The usual tricks were tried to conquer his habit. Mrs. Sweet had restricted his fluids at supper time. She had awakened and escorted the sleepy-eyed boy to the bathroom several times a night. She rewarded, bribed, humiliated him in turn without success. In disgust, she put the soaked sheets and pajamas aside for Ronnie to wash.

After medications and sleep-alarm devices didn't improve his bladder control, his family arranged for me to see him. Mrs. Sweet walking ahead of her son, notebook in hand, acknowledged my greeting with a nod. She started right in.

"He's a changed boy, Doctor. Something has to be done about his wetting. A child his age. I don't understand it. It's affecting his school work. Why, he used to get all A's. No more. He'll be lucky to pass."

"I see. Has he missed much time from school this year?"

"No. He was there every day. For all the good it did."

"Is he pretty active? Does he like to ride his bike, swim, play ball?"

"Oh, yes. That he'll do."

"Appetite good?"

"Ravenous."

"Any change in weight?"

"Matter of fact, he's lost some weight. Even though he's at the refrigerator all the time."

"Did you mention this to your other doctor?"

"No. We just talked on the phone. I didn't take Ronnie to see him."

"Has anyone else in the family had this problem? Parents, brothers, sister and so on?"

"I should say not! He's the only one and I'll tell you, I can't take it much longer."

Ronnie sat through her lamentations. He appeared cowed by his outraged mother. He probably wondered if I would be added to the list of those who thought he wet his bed every night because he was lazy, or that he did it on purpose. He never told her that he often would stay awake, fighting sleep, because he dreaded the discovery of another failure on his part.

The examination didn't give me a clue as to why Ronnie had reverted to bed-wetting. But in talking to him, I learned that he had to run to the toilet many times during the day as well. His teacher insisted that he wait until recess and so he suffered the ridicule of his classmates when he couldn't hold back.

It didn't come as a surprise when his urinalysis showed four plus sugar and four plus acetone. Simple explanation. The famous old medical maxim was right again. When you have the three P's—polyphagia, polydypsia and polyuria—look for the fourth P, the urine.

"Mrs. Sweet, we should be able to help him keep his bed dry."

"That's wonderful! You're going to give him something for his nerves? I should take something too. This hasn't been easy on me, you know."

I held up my hand. "Hold on. His nerves have nothing to do with it. Ronnie has diabetes. As soon as we do some blood tests, we can get him back in shape."

Ronnie was an apt student and quickly learned to give himself insulin and monitored his doses by home testing of blood sugar levels. He knew about the high carbohydrate foods and didn't mind skipping the pastries and candies, as long as he escaped the shame of a drenched bed.

But his family couldn't accept the life-long commitment to insulin and diet. They looked for other answers. Ronnie missed one appointment after another. They didn't bother to cancel.

There must be an underground news gathering system. Dr. Howley's name reached the Sweets' ears through this word-of-mouth network. Ronnie's mother was entranced when she was told by one of the doctor's followers that insulin would not be necessary and that herbal prescriptions would be the main treatment.

Dr. Howley's offices occupied the entire first floor of a modern, three-story building in the center of the town. He was a thin man, in his early thirties, dressed in a loose-fitting robe with a tassel instead of a belt. He wore sandals and had heavy necklaces. No stethoscope. His voice was soft and soothing as he assured Mrs. Sweet that Ronnie would be whole again if he followed his suggestions.

No one thought about his credentials. His promises satisfied them. There were no diplomas, no license posted, nothing to verify his medical background. Dr. Howley, in fact, had dropped out of high school after his second year. He had worked in carnivals, in burlesque theaters, in discount stores. He had studied people and was conscious of their gullibility. Gradually he perfected his presentation. No raucous barking out the wonders on the midway, no merchandising a product from the back of a station wagon. His approach was more subtle.

He adopted the doctor title and went from store to store, buying equipment with impressive cabinets and switches that could make his machinery hum or blink with a flick of his finger. His consultation room was furnished with thick Oriental rugs, subdued lighting, a stereo sound system and a number of potted plants. In lieu of the usual credentials, there were framed photostats of letters from the many he had cured, hung at random on the paneled walls.

At the first interview with his patients, Dr. Howley made it clear that he was blessed with a rare healing skill, not based on traditional medicine, but on knowledge extracted from ancient writings, from his own investigations and from divine inspiration. He would not accept payment for his services because he was being guided by a higher source. His receptionist, he explained, was in charge of voluntary donations. They were to be given to the "Sacred Tabernacle," his religious order, and she would be happy to suggest an appropriate amount for his health mission.

Annie Mae, too, was taken in by the young "doctor's" manner. He seemed to understand how much she had suffered and assured her there would be an end to her distress. Massage, sulfur waters, vitamin tablets and weekly sessions with the "Cosmic Current" machine would allow her to live free of pain and disease. She had a radiance Sal hadn't seen in years.

Ronnie, also, responded to Dr. Howley's unorthodox methods. Most of the nights his bed was dry. He would be able to go to overnight camp and leave the rubber sheet behind, and so his mother enrolled him for four weeks at the Sacred Tabernacle's summer program. Dr. Howley and a staff of counselors operated a wilderness project for their patients. Swimming, baseball, hiking, mountain climbing and meditation were featured, along with meals prepared by his cooks.

The camp's fifty-acre site was in a remote area, miles from the nearest town. A single, winding, unpaved road was the only access from the main highway, and four-wheel-drive vehicles were needed for deliveries of mail and basic supplies. The children were bused from his urban office, and parents were not allowed to visit. One phone call a week was sanctioned but limited to five minutes, no exceptions.

Ronnie had been away for two weeks when I received a call from a community hospital about seventy miles away from his camp. The intern asked to speak to me right away.

"Doctor, I have a patient of yours. A youngster from that summer camp. He's in a diabetic coma, and I need some information. Can you help me?"

"Who's the child?" I asked. "I don't have any juvenile diabetics under active treatment now. I wonder how you got my name?"

"Got it from his family. Someone dropped this sick kid, Ronnie Sweet, in our laps. No history, nothing. A jeep from that screwy place in the woods came here this morning. Some fellow in a gown brought him to us. Gave us a slip of paper with his folk's phone number and took off. Said he had to get back to his flock. That's what he said, his flock. If we needed any advice, we should call him. Can you beat that?"

"I'm surprised they gave you my name. I'll help all I can. Ronnie was under my care until a few months ago. That's when they found this Dr. Howley. He's a faith healer, I guess. I understand he took Ronnie off insulin and started treating the diabetes his own way."

The intern's whistle came shrilly across the lines.

"Doctor, this boy's blood sugar was out of sight, over 800 milligrams and his ketosis is just starting to come around after a liter of lactated Ringer's and insulin. He needed plenty to control him. We got the permits over the phone. The hospital administrator witnessed the consent."

"It sounds as if you're doing fine, Doctor. Why did you call me?"

"Well, once we get him regulated, we don't know what to do with him. The parents told us they want us to send him back to that Sacred Tabernacle camp. It doesn't seem safe. This kid'll get in trouble without insulin. And those characters aren't doctors. They're dangerous."

"I know how you feel. But his parents have the right to have anyone they want take care of him. They seem to believe everything this Howley tells them."

"He's a quack, pure and simple."

"Document everything you told me," I suggested. "I mean how Ronnie got to the hospital. Write it up and send it to me. There are some other Howley cases in town that need a good review by the authorities. But you have to have witnesses and signatures on the records you send. O.K?"

"What can I say? I'll do it. The hospital chief will make sure we get it all neatly done. We'll send Ronnie back to that camp when he's under better control."

Sal called to me from Annie Mae's hospital room a week or so later.

"How about saying hello to Annie May, Doc? She's in here for surgery. They'll be operating tomorrow and she's scared stiff. I know she'll feel better if you can visit for a little while."

"Gee, Sal, someone said she was doing fine. That the new doctor, that Dr. Howley, was working wonders."

"He was at first. She was gettin' out of bed and stayin' out most of the day. Hadn't done that in a couple of years. Those ray treatments were giving her pep, or maybe it was the pills and herbs."

I looked in on Annie Mae. She was sitting in a chair near the window. She looked like a Buddha or a bullfrog with her puffed-out belly, breathless and even more frightened than usual. A few reassuring words from me brought a little smile to her lips. She rubbed her huge abdomen. "I was much better until Dr. Howley left for his camp. I could feel the tumor in my insides getting smaller."

She reached for Sal's calloused hand.

"Sal took me out shopping. We went to that new mall right outside of town. He waited in the truck 'cause I wanted to shop alone. Would've been the first time in over two years that I'd done the groceries."

Annie Mae paused for breath. "I got out of the cab—down that high step. I started to walk slowly to the store. Doctor, I lost my balance and landed flat on my back. There was no way I could get up by myself. I screamed for Sal . . . he doesn't hear too well. A couple of men had to lift me to my feet. They called the rescue squad, and here I am."

Sal broke in, "Annie Mae, I'm going to walk the doctor to the elevator. I'll be right back, honey."

He stopped when we reached the elevator doors. "Do you mind if I ask you a favor? I hate to, but this trouble with Annie Mae . . ."

"If I can help, I'll be glad to. What do you need?"

"An extra job, Doctor. The surgery is going to cost a bundle. I'm happy that it'll take care of her trouble. Wish she'd seen to it a long time ago."

"Sal," I said, "I can let you take whatever you need."

"Oh, no, not in a million years. I couldn't borrow from you. I thought, though, I could work weekends at your place. Build the patio you wanted. Remember I couldn't find the time then. But Dr. Howley's treatments were awfully high."

"Really? I thought he didn't have fees. People could give him what they could afford."

"The lady at the desk said that. But she suggested seventy-five dollars each time would be fair, because Annie Mae was so sick."

"Do you owe him much?"

Sal shook his head. "Not a penny. I paid cash every time. Toward the end, before he left for his camp, Annie Mae went twice a week. You see, he was worried that the tumor would grow bigger while he was away."

"Sal, he's not a doctor. You know that, don't you? Are you satisfied he was helping your wife?"

"Oh, yes. He's a wonderful person. It was as he said. When he had to be away, that swelling came right back."

"Sal," I said, "someone could have kept up treatments while he was gone. Didn't you ask him? Other doctors do that for my patients while I'm on vacation."

"We called from the hospital the day Annie Mae was admitted. No answer at his office and the lady at the summer place said he couldn't be interrupted. He was praying."

I pressed the button for the elevator. "Any time you want to start on my patio is fine with us. Probably will take a couple of weekends if the weather cooperates. Would you like me to pay in advance?"

"No. I don't think I'll need it right away. I want to have something in reserve for later, when Dr. Howley comes back. Annie Mae liked him."

The hospital records concerning Ronnie's admission for diabetic coma were far more frightening than I thought possible. He had been discharged against the hospital's advice to the Sacred Tabernacle's camp. The same scene was repeated less than a week later. Ronnie was rushed back in critical condition again. It took longer to correct his distorted sugar metabolism.

This time, however, the sheriff was called to force Dr. Howley to leave the hospital. When he was questioned by the same intern about his absurd way of dealing with a diabetic child, he had become abusive. He began to shout, I was told, and insisted that Ronnie's difficulties came because the doctors had not followed his advice.

"Coffee enemas every day, that'll bring the sugar down. Shots never cured anybody. That young man (he had pointed to the intern) wouldn't let me tell him about putting watermelon juice in the intravenous drip. I've cured dozens of diabetics with coffee enemas and the IV's. I don't have the set-up yet at my camp, but you can bet that next year this won't happen!"

The orderlies had to restrain Dr. Howley until the sheriff's deputy led him away from the hospital.

At the request of the hospital administrator, I forwarded a report of Ronnie's unhappy experience, as well as a copy of the pathologist's analysis of the ovarian tumor the surgeon removed from Annie Mae. An investigation by the district attorney's office was conducted, but neither Ronnie's parents nor Annie Mae would testify against Dr. Howley. Both continued under the guidance of the self-appointed healer.

The State Licensing Board tried to restrain him from practicing without a license. But his lawyer successfully countered that he was the head of an order, the Sacred Tabernacle, and as the spiritual counselor to hundreds or people, both healthy and ailing, he needed no such sanction.

❧

Once your mind begins to float, it's hard to tell where it will light. I had been drifting in and out of reveries, going through the time warp of my career. The trip had been worth taking, even with the injustice of the arsenic poisoning lawsuit. I knew that I would continue to be a part of the lullabies and nightmares in the lives of my patients.